McMILLEN's

TEXAS GARDENING
Wildflowers

Publisher/President — Rick McMillen
Vice President/Chief Financial Officer — Marna McMillen
Vice President/Director of Publishing Operations — Sir McMillen
Business Manager — Bobbye Jean Smith
Executive Assistant — Stormy Waters
Executive Editor — Jim Carley
Senior Editor/Writer — Paul Cox
Research Editor — Jim Walden
Editorial Assistant — Kevin Newberry
Contributors — Janis Merritt, Kerry Blackmon, Jim Molony, Jim Walden, Laura Friedman, Jennifer Condi

Creative Director — Jeff Wolf
Design/Graphics — Cheryl Leary
Design/Graphics Assistant — David Medina
Production — Aaron Brittain
Photography — Courtesy San Antonio Botanical Gardens, Lady Bird Johnson Wildflower Center, Texas Department of Transportation, Vickie McMillen
Cover Photo — Courtesy San Antonio Botanical Gardens

Circulation Manager — Bambi McMillen
Data Processing Coordinator — James Porter
Data Processing — Danette Daniel, Erin Folks, Adrian Jackson, Kudirat Muhammed, Jessica Ortega, Vikki Singley, Diane Thorne

Advertising Director — Al Allen
Corporate Sales Director — Harvey Hooker
Advertising Coordinator — Tiffany McMillen
Sales Representative/Houston —Al Allen
http://www.mcmillencomm.com

© *1998 Gulf Publishing Company*
3301 Allen Parkway, Houston TX 77019
P.O. Box 2608, Houston, TX 77252
http://www.gulfpub.com/books.html

ISBN# 0-88415-894-2
Gulf Publishing Company

AURORA

"The Roman Goddess of Dawn"
— Webster's Unabridged Dictionary

Wildflowers ... they spring up each year, vibrant and colorful begging you
without phrase to enjoy. No commitment required except for the visual pleasure
and the unmistakable fragrance that captures your unexpected senses.
You watch them sway gently, being caressed by the warm and inviting spring
breezes ... and your mind is left with an aimless peacefulness.
Each time I see *Aurora*, my granddaughter, I am
overwhelmed with her uncomplicated beauty.
And like *Wildflowers* ... there are no rules — simply enjoy me PaPaw
and I will enjoy you. She too is vibrant and colorful with nothing ever spoken
that is near understandable ... yet we relate. Much like the *Wildflowers*,
she will be enjoyed simply for her quiet beauty without the
complications which become part of all adult lives.
If I am to be charged with the responsibility of publishing a book
about one of the true gifts of the gods — *Wildflowers* — then I must
dedicate it to another equally magnificent gift from the gods — *Aurora*.
Your grandfather simply adores you,
PaPaw
Rick McMillen, Publisher

Paul Cox

Paul Cox is the acting director of the San Antonio Botanical Gardens where he has worked in various capacities for more than 20 years. He holds a B.S. and M.S. from Stephen F. Austin University.

He is the senior author of *Texas Trees — A Friendly Guide*, which has won two awards and is now in its sixth printing.

Janis Merritt

Janis Merritt has worked at the San Antonio Botanical Gardens for more than seven years. She earned her degree in horticulture from Palo Alto College in San Antonio. She is currently curator of the native areas at the Gardens. Her outreach to the community includes teaching con-tinuing education classes. She also con-sults with local schools and surrounding city governments on wildscaping, butterfly gardening and xeriscaping. She also writes a monthly article on the Plant of the Month for the *San Antonio Gardener* newsletter published by the San Antonio Master Gardeners.

Jim Molony

Jim Molony is editor-in-chief of the *Bay Area Sun* and *Mariner's Log* newspapers in Webster, Texas. He is a Houston-based, free-lance writer whose interest in botany dates back to his days at the University of Houston.

Table of Contents

MYSTERIES OF THE TEXAS BLUEBONNET

By PAUL COX
Acting Director
San Antonio Botanical Center

In the long and fanciful history of the beloved Texas bluebonnet, it sometimes seems there are almost more stories and myths than there are flowers.

And the stories must begin with the controversy surrounding the naming of the beautiful prolific plant as the official state flower. After the dust of the "flower wars" settled, Texas ended up with five state flowers.

The subject is so dear to the hearts of Texans that the state legislature almost never came to a determination on which bluebonnet to be the official flower. There are no fewer than five different species of the bluebonnet and all are official state flowers.

That confusion began in the spring of 1901 when the state legislature was seeking a state flower and such diverse plants as the cotton boll — since cotton was then king in Texas — and the cactus were placed in nomination.

Judge John M. Green of Cuero, influenced by some "club women from Dallas," championed the cause of making the buffalo clover or bluebonnet, the official Texas state flower. He expected the measure to sail through the legislature unopposed and was surprised when amendments were proposed to use the "open cotton ball or white rose of commerce."

This is one of the five species of bluebonnets that has caused on-going controversy in the Texas Legislature.

Another group wanted to strike out buffalo clover and insert "cactus" as the official Texas state flower.

A third counter-proposal was the "cotton bloom" rather than the open ball.

The debate finally settled in between the open cotton ball and the

San Antonio Botanical Center Photo

bluebonnet. Cotton was put forth as the source of great wealth since Texas probably led the world in exported cotton. Green argued that "the basic idea for having a state flower was sentimental," and they should choose something that "grew wild and free on our hillsides and broad prairies," not something that suggested "toil and grime and sweat and losses."

Fortunately for the state, Green and the National Society of Colonial Dames of America in Texas helped convince the legislators that the bluebonnet was the floral emblem for them. Problem was, the judge and the ladies had lobbied for the lupinus subcarnosus, a dainty flower that primarily covers hills and beaches in southern Texas. Unfortunately for the legislature, many Texans felt that bluebonnet was the least attractive of the Texas bluebonnets and botanists and serious gardeners around the state

Is it a Crime to Pick 'Em?

An often asked question: Is picking roadside bluebonnets against the law as is commonly believed? Will state troopers storm the area, put you in handcuffs and whisk you off to jail if you're caught grabbing a few bluebonnets in your fist while sitting at a roadside park?

Surprisingly, the answer is no.

But digging them up is against the law.

The Texas Department of Public Safety's official stance is that picking a handful of blossoms is allowable, but digging up or otherwise destroying the plants is unlawful.

Still, picking many flowers is not encouraged as they should be left for all to enjoy their natural beauty.

began their battles to dislodge lupinus subcarnosus.

Soon a faction developed encouraging the legislature to adopt the Texas bluebonnet, lupinus texensis. This is the species that grows throughout most of Texas and the one popularized by Texas artists. And that was just the beginning of the battle.

For 70 years the bluebonnet debate continued until 1971, when the legislature acquiesced and solved the problem by adding a covering clause that included both species and "any other variety of bluebonnet not heretofore recorded." This also added the three other native species, so all five became the official Texas state flower. The new additions were: lupinus texensis, which is found growing naturally in central Texas. It's the most popular and easily cultivated of the native species. Lupinus havardii, the Big Bend bluebonnet, is the largest of our natives, reaching heights of

San Antonio Botanical Center Photo

The Texas bluebonnet is the most pictured flower in our state and second only to the state silhouette as an emblem of recognition.

three feet or more. In Texas, it's confined to lower elevations in Hudspeth, Presidio and Brewster counties. Lupinus concinnus is the least conspicuous plant with small white, lavender and pink flowers. It's found at elevations above 4,500 feet in west Texas. Lupinus plattensis, which grows to about two feet tall, is rare in the sandy soils of Hartley County in the Panhandle. It is our only native perennial lupine.

The genus name lupinus is derived from the Latin word for wolf, lupus. In antiquity, lupines were called wolf flowers for it was thought that they devoured the dirt because the plants were often found in areas of thin soil. Today it is recognized that lupines are usually pioneers on recently exposed sites. The name buffalo clover comes from the affinity these plants had for the edges of buffalo wallows where the soil was distributed providing them with a favorable seed bed.

Native Americans also were fond of the flower and had many myths and legends surrounding it. Probably the most popular and sentimental is the story of the Comanche village that was suffering during a long, terrible drought.

The village's spiritual leaders said word had come from the Great Spirits that in order to alleviate the dry spell, the villagers must sacrifice their most valued possessions. But the selfish people were reluctant to relinquish their most prized articles.

One night as the village slept on its predicament, a little orphan girl named

She-Who-Is-Alone knew what to do. She took her most prized possession, a warrior doll decorated with Blue Jay feathers, to the top of a hill. There she burned the doll as a sacrifice and scattered the ashes in the wind.

The next morning the awakening tribe was astonished to see bright blue flowers covering the hill where the doll's ashes had fallen. The little girl's heroic sacrifice had gained the Great Spirits' approval and rain began to fall ending the drought.

Local Mexican natives often referred to lupinus texensis as 'el conejo' or the rabbit, because the flowers were tipped with white, reminding them of a bunny's tail.

One of the things the bluebonnet had going for it was its cultural mystique. Other wildflowers are comparatively easy to cultivate. For years, propagation of the Texas bluebonnet was shrouded in ceremony and ritual.

It was thought that bluebonnet seeds needed to variously be soaked, boiled, frozen, forgotten or impaled with a pin. The idea behind all this horticultural ju-ju was to soften the pebble-hard seed coat.

After they germinated, it was thought that the seedlings needed to be inoculated with a bacteria known as rhizobium. This was supposed to enable the plant to convert soil minerals into available nutrients. Actually these legumes help enrich the soil by adding nitrogen from their roots.

With all these requirements, it's a wonder the plants could survive in the wild. That seems oddly contradictive in that the wildflower of a state known for

San Antonio Botanical Center Photo

The lupinus subcarnosus was the lone original state flower

its rugged reputation requires such delicate treatment to grow. The popularization of the Texas bluebonnet as a cultivated ornamental wildflower can be traced directly to the efforts of two men — Carroll Abbott and Dr. Jerry Parsons.

Abbott, "Mr. Texas Bluebonnet," was born in 1926 in Texarkana, but moved to Houston while still an infant. He was interested in wildflowers from an early age. During the depression, he dug and sold plants to help support the family. In some weeks he actually made more income than his father, a Baptist minister and handy man.

In 1948, his parents moved to Kerrville. The four acres they purchased now has a bronze plaque affixed to a boulder commemorating his accomplishments.

Abbott worked in the media where he honed his communication skills all the while maintaining his plant interests, growing many in his back yard, often in metal cans. By 1961, he was running political campaigns for several members of the state Democratic party.

San Antonio Botanical Center Photo

Lupinus texensis is the most popular and easily cultivated of the native species.

In one of John Connally's campaigns, Abbott once sent out 10,000 promotional seed packages.

During his travels around the state, Abbott kept journals recording his wildflower observations. It was Abbott who noted bluebonnets developed a red spot in the middle after they had been pollinated. He began to grow concerned about the apparent decline in wildflowers, largely due to construction, development and poor management techniques. In 1970, he resigned at the height of his success and devoted the rest of his life to his first passion — wildflowers.

Since relatively few native wild-flower seeds were available, he established his seed company called Green Horizons. Bluebonnet seed sales were his bread and butter during the austere early years of the company. He pioneered efforts to expedite the germination of bluebonnet seeds and while his methods were somewhat crude by today's standards, he succeeded in achieving seeds that had relatively uniform and rapid germination. This was accomplished by churning of seeds in a cement mixer with coarse sand, the basic idea being to soften the rock hard seed coat barrier so that moisture could penetrate more readily.

In 1976, he began a quarterly

newsletter promoting native plants and how to care for them. This was so unique and well written he was awarded the Golden Quill Award by the Men's Garden Club of America.

In 1978, he published the book *How to Know and Grow Texas Wildflowers*, which finally sold out in 1981. That same year he helped Texas Woman's University in Denton restore its wildflower garden. It had been started in 1930, but had since fallen into disrepair. His work with TWU led to the first Wildflower Day, held in the spring of 1980. Later Abbott was one of the founders of the Native Plant Society of Texas, which first met on April 25, 1981.

Abbott was diagnosed with cancer in 1981 and given the President's award by the NPSOT in 1983. Lady Bird Johnson received the award for him as Abbott was too ill to attend. He died July 6, 1984.

During his research, Abbott's efforts caught the imagination of Bexar County State Agriculture Extension Agent Dr. Jerry Parsons. The saga began in 1982 when Parsons and Dr. Steve George did a live television broadcast at the San Antonio Botanical Center on sowing Abbott's treated bluebonnet seed and raking them into soil.

It was a simple demonstration, but the audience response was incredible. The TV station was totally overwhelmed by callers wanting to know where they could obtain these fast germinating bluebonnet seeds.

This prompted Parsons to pay Abbott a visit and they quickly became fast friends. Abbott shared his dream of having a 1986 sesquicentennial flag planting composed of nothing but bluebonnets. Inspired by this idea, Parsons began a dogged campaign to realize Abbott's sesquicentennial dream. Parson's aggressive pursuit of this project was both energetic and resourceful.

How To Grow Them

Gardeners today have bluebonnets available as bedding plants or pretreated seed offered in several color variations and with reliable germination.

They are reasonably easy to grow as long as some basic rules are followed. Seeds need to be chemically scarified and planted no later than September 15 in the Dallas-Fort Worth area and by Thanksgiving in the San Antonio vicinity.

Transplants can be placed out later, Halloween is the deadline in North Texas and Valentines Day in South Texas. They perform best in one foot on center spacings.

Plant them in full sun in well drained soil using pretreated seed just below the soil surface. Don't plant transplants lower than their crown or they'll rot. Don't over-water but only apply when the top inch of soil is dry.

Fertilizing isn't required but will give more abundant blooms.

San Antonio Botanical Center Photo

In 1971, the Texas State Legislature passed an amendment stating that the state flower would include "any other variety of bluebonnet not heretofore recorded."

He realized that such a feat couldn't be accomplished by casually sowing the seeds and hoping for the best. They would have to be planted as transplants. Seedlings might germinate readily, but they are the most vulnerable and delicate in their juvenile stage. Transplants would be hardier and easier to space in order to achieve a formal design.

He first discovered that uniform germination could be obtained by treating the seed with sulfuric acid. This was achieved by several years of costly trial and error.

Sowing seeds is easy, so it is most popular. However, it often produces erratic or unreliable plantings because of some procedural error. Transplants,

on the other hand, offer a reliable plant properly timed and spaced. Parsons worked with Peterson Brothers nursery in San Antonio and together they produced the first commercially available bluebonnet bedding plant in 1983. That has since developed into a multi-million dollar industry. The next step was more challenging.

Abbott knew he had seen isolated individuals in large bluebonnet populations that represented the color variations he desired. Although many had seen the white bluebonnet, there were those who claimed the existence of pink and red bluebonnets were a myth. Parsons took Abbott's information and through an imaginative and tireless campaign utiliz-

San Antonio Botanical Center Photo

Today it is possible to obtain garden transplants offering a wide range of bluebonnet color selections.

ing his media and agricultural connections, he managed to select and grow in quantity many different color variations of lupinus texensis.

The search for an "albino" bluebonnet began with a television broadcast on Feb. 30, 1984. On March 29, 1985, the public search for a pink bluebonnet was aired.

Pink bluebonnets proved to be so rare that only four locations were found in the entire state with the largest population occurring within the San Antonio city limits. Perpetuating the pink strain proved to be somewhat difficult as the first season yielded only 12 percent pink seedlings.

Whites, by comparison, yielded 75

percent true to color. Recognizing the special nature of the pink selection, Parsons named it after its mentor — the Abbott pink. Parsons' work was not finished and later he developed many color strains. This included white, pink, lavender and, eventually, a deep maroon. Surprisingly, many experts openly criticized his efforts. This only made him more determined and by 1986, he had partially realized the goal and had production numbers of blue, white and pink. The red didn't come until later.

Today it is possible to obtain garden transplants offering a wide range of bluebonnet color selections. One tangential controversy this set in motion is the proper naming of these plants. Are they white, pink or red bonnets? The answer is bluebonnet is one word so there are different variations of this plant.

An unforeseen situation developed as some experts renounced Parson's efforts claiming he was a Dr. Frankenstein meddling in the sacred laws of nature by creating unnatural hybrids using our beloved state flower. Actually these are not hybrids in any sense of the word but naturally occurring variations that are painstakingly selected and perpetuated.

Parsons' bluebonnet work didn't cease once he had reached the sesquicentennial goal. Now that the germinating secrets were unlocked, a flood of possibilities were released.

He eventually patented the use of the Big Bend bluebonnet, always considered the most difficult to grow, as a long stem cutflower.

All of this work was accomplished with no more staff than a few individuals such as his co-workers, George and Greg Grant, a large media following that actively searched for the different color strains and the cooperation of a few farmers who donated portions of their valuable agricultural fields.

Another person who is instrumental in popularizing our state flower is John Thomas of Wildseed Farms Inc. He took a small seat-of-the-pants operation near Eagle Lake and turned it into a multi-million dollar business.

His efforts are partially responsible for the beautiful wildflower displays we see today along many of Texas' highways. He also helped Parsons by offering portions of his crop fields to

perpetuate some of the many bluebonnet color selections.

Texans have always been vain about their state emblems. The tree is the pecan, the state bird is the mockingbird, the state gem stone is Texas blue topaz, the state rock is petrified palm wood and there's even a state grass — side oats grama.

While these are all great in their own right, none swells a Texan's pride quite like the state flower — the bluebonnet. ❀

San Antonio Botanical Center Photo

No state emblem swells a Texan's pride like the bluebonnet.

RECAPTURING THE PRAIRIES IN YOUR BACKYARD

By JANIS MERRITT
Native Plant Curator
San Antonio Botanical
Gardens

The wildflowers you see on the side of the road today were once part of the vast prairies which covered millions of acres of Texas. Through stories handed down from the early pioneers, we have learned that much of Texas was prairie punctuated with only a scattering of trees, those mainly along streams.

Early settlers described with awe the prairie as a sea of green with flowers of every color.

Few prairies remain today, but we can still capture some of what those pioneers saw by planting a little prairie in our own backyards.

In pioneer days, the prairies supported between 200 and 400 different species of plants. Fifty-to-80 percent of those were grasses with wildflowers growing between their clumps. Wildflowers evolved with grasses which held them up as they strove to attract pollinators.

The diversity of wildflowers attracts

San Antonio Botanical Center Photo

The gay-feather is a common prairie plant cultivated in your backyard.

numerous types of insects which become an important part of the diet for birds, especially in the spring when they are feeding their young. Due to the early blooming period of wildflowers, they're also an important source of nectar for butterflies and returning hummingbirds.

Bluebonnets, firewheels, and purple horsemint are some of the annuals you see in a wildflower meadow. When a site is disturbed, it is the annuals that make the first appearance. Annuals germinate, grow, bloom, set seed and die all within a one-year period.

The annuals continue to occupy this site until they improve the soil for perennials to move in. This comes after successive years of the soil-enriching process of dying plants and nitrogen-fixing legumes.

Perennials live for several years and develop a deep root system. Food reserves in their roots allow them to grow quickly in the spring, shading out the annuals.

Once a prairie has reached its climax, it becomes weed resistant, drought tolerant and continues to improve the soil in which it grows.

There are three types of prairie — tallgrass, mixed and shortgrass. Tallgrass prairies are found on wetter sites which could also support trees, but periodic fires started by lightning or intentionally set by Native Americans maintained the rich grasslands and wildlife it supported.

Bison that once roamed Texas in great herds also affected the prairie. Their hooves would disturb the soil and cut the large clumps of grass into several smaller clumps. They would heavily graze the grasses, then move on, leaving behind fertilizer to recycle the nutrients. The four major components of a tallgrass prairie are switchgrass, indiangrass, big bluestem and little bluestem. As you move further west where there is less precipitation, the mixed prairie can be found.

The mixed prairie is comprised of some of the plants from both the tallgrass and shortgrass prairie. The shortgrass prairie is found under more arid conditions.

Buffalo grass and blue grama are indicators of the shortgrass prairie and are finding their way into our landscapes as drought tolerant turf alternatives.

As gardeners we can help to preserve our prairie heritage by planting a pocket prairie in our own backyards. There are several things to consider to increase your chances of a successful wildflower meadow.

One of the most important considerations is site selection. Select a site that is well-drained and will not stay too wet for long periods of time. Moist sites will usually contain too many weedy species and not provide enough oxygen in the soil for a healthy root system.

Eliminate competition from aggressive weeds or alien species. Alien species such as clover, winter rye and johnson grass are too aggressive and will compete for space, nutrients and water. Prairie wildflowers need at least eight hours of sunlight a day or they will become leggy and produce fewer flowers.

The best time to plant is in the spring or fall when rainfall is more abundant. In the fall, sow spring and summer blooming plants. In the spring, sow fall blooming wildflowers. If you wish to include native grass seed in your meadow, the best time to plant it is in the spring.

Properly select plants for your area and site. Determine what you want in your wildflower meadow and what look you are trying to achieve. If you are not sure which plants will do best, start first with a small area and get a variety of plant seed that you desire.

San Antonio Botanical Center Photo

Standing cypress is a favorite choice for home gardens.

This will allow you to see which species best suits your site. What does well in your site may differ from your neighbors site. Purchase seed that is grown and collected in your bio-region. Plants from these seeds will be better adapted to your soil, temperature range and rainfall. Sow seeds at the recommended seeding rate for best results. It is better to have too many seed in a smaller area than not enough seed over a large area.

Once you have made your site selection and purchased your seed you are ready to do the site preparation. First, mow all existing vegetation in the area to be planted; rake and remove the debris.

Second, you must slightly loosen the soil. This can be done by raking, lightly tilling or disking the area. Don't go deeper than one inch as this will allow dormant weed seeds buried in the soil to germinate and become an uncontrollable problem.

Next, you are ready to sow your wildflower seeds. For a more even distribution, mix your wildflower seed with sand using one part seed to four parts sand. Use a bucket-and-hand-broadcasting system or a fertilizer spreader and walk back and forth until you have covered the area to be planted with half of the seed. Then sow the remaining half of seed walking back and forth perpendicular to the initial sowing. This will ensure an even distribution of seed and eliminate stripes created by missed strips.

In order for the seed to germinate and grow, the seed must make good contact with the soil. After sowing your seed, rolling or walking to press the seed into the soil is essential for planting success. If you have sown large seed, you might wish to lightly rake the seed into the soil before rolling. There will still be seed visible. If you have small seed, you can skip this process as the rolling alone will be sufficient.

Keeping the wildflower meadow moist for four-to-six weeks is critical after planting. How often you will have to water will depend on the amount of rainfall you receive and your type of soil. Water frequently but lightly until the seedlings have reached a height of one-to-two inches. Gradually reduce the amount of watering. If there is a long dry period between rainfall, water infrequently and deeper to encourage a deeper root system.

If you are planting a large area and are unable to irrigate, the amount of rainfall you receive will determine the success of your wildflower meadow. Time your planting carefully to take advantage of your rainy season. A wet year will yield more favorable results than a dry year.

Proper planning and planting will go far in producing the wildflower meadow you desire. However, the importance of maintenance can not be overlooked.

Remove weeds before they go to seed to keep them from getting out of control. After all the wildflowers have gone to seed, wait at least two weeks before mowing. At this time the meadow will look a little ragged, but allowing the seed to mature and disperse before mowing will keep you from having to purchase more seed and start all over the following year. If you have sown perennials in the meadow, mow at a height of at least four-to-six inches to prevent damage to your plants.

A wildflower mixture of annuals and perennials will give you color the first year of planting. Allow perennials two or three years to produce flowers. Remember that climatic conditions such as drought, floods and hail play an important role in the success and dynamics of a wildflower meadow. Wet years will favor some species in your meadow making them more abundant one year and less abundant in dry years.

Plan to devote some time and a lot of patience in developing a pocket prairie. It took Mother Nature thousands of years to create Texas prairies which we try to duplicate in just a few years. Original prairies evolved with hundreds of species of plants and a close interaction with insects and animals.

San Antonio Botanical Center Photo

Bluebonnets and Indian paint brushes are among the most popular plants to cultivate.

Fire kept woody plants from encroaching onto the prairie and returned nutrients to the soil. Great herds of bison grazed on the prairie grasses, recycling it with natural fertilizer. Then they moved on to allow the grasses to recover and bloom and the resulting seed would fall to the slightly disturbed ground. In the absence of fire and bison, mowing and selectively removing woody plants is useful in maintaining our young wildflower meadows.

The rewards of planting a prairie lie in its mystery and ever-changing display of color. Observe closely the insects, butterflies and birds that will be drawn closer and make all your efforts worthwhile. ❁

LADY BIRD'S WILDFLOWER CENTER IN FULL BLOOM

"The idea of a research center for North American native plants went tantalizingly around in my mind. And finally I decided that, in this happy time of my life, this would be the project I would give my time and energy to."
— *Lady Bird Johnson*
at dedication of National
Wildflower Research Center, 1982.

By JIM MOLONY

Lady Bird Johnson's dream of a wildflower research center has grown far beyond the humble origins she had envisioned as a national resource for native plant information when the for-

mer first lady turned the first shovel of earth on a 60-acre piece of property in northeast Austin that would be known as the National Wildflower Research Center. Since then, the center has moved and as of March 1998, is known as the Lady Bird Johnson Wildflower Center.

The new 42-acre site, which opened in 1995, is on a rolling-hill tract on the northern fringe of the city. Though smaller than the original, it has become a Mecca for wildflower enthusiasts and research personnel. In 1997, more than 120,000 people toured the grounds, the third consecutive year the still-under-construction facility has enjoyed

Wildflower Center Photo — Carl Pingrey

Irises are highlighted in the front-gate water feature at the Lady Bird Johnson Wildflower Center.

increased attendance.

"People are generally surprised their first time here, but then it was the same way at the original site," Julie Barrett Heffington, LBJWC Director of Gardens and Education, said. "The original site was a very humble setting, absolutely nothing like this."

The original site between Del Valle and Manor was donated by the Johnson family.

"It was meant to be a research area, not a public site, but people kept stopping by wanting to know what we were doing, and eventually display gardens were set up and volunteers were brought in to teach the public about what we were doing," Heffington said. "It wasn't long until it became obvious and evident that that real role of the center was dissemination of information and to really show how native plants can benefit the environment."

The center maintains one of the largest collections of information about native North American plants and makes this information available to more than 23,000 members across the continent as well as landscape professionals and gardeners around the world.

A visit to the new center underscores that mission. From the moment you walk in, the natural beauty is obvious. And unlike many botanical gardens, where the flora is contrived, the staff at the LBJWC have meticulously maintained the natural setting. Everything is native to Central Texas, from the plants and wildlife to the materials used in the construction of the facility.

"The sandstone comes from Lampasas, the limestone from Comfort and the flagstone comes from Dryden," LBJWC assistant director Patricia Alholm said.

"Even the planking and materials for the visitors' gallery are recycled from buildings in the area."

The buildings are environmentally conscious in design yet functional to the LBJWC's stated goals of applying nature's principles to created landscapes. One example of the center's strict adherence to environmentally sound projects is the watering system.

Wildflower Center Photo — Josh Blumenfield

Ralph the talking lawnmower entertains children in the visitor's gallery.

Wildflower Center Photo

**The observation tower looks out over
one of 23 showy display gardens.**

Not wishing to tap the Edwards Aquifer, another method had to be found to water the center's plants during periods of drought. A rooftop rainwater harvesting program, the largest of its kind in North America, was included in the facility's design. The system is designed to collect enough rainwater to fill all of the center's irrigation needs.

The tin roofs on all of the buildings drain into water features, where the water is re-circulated or routed into three cisterns. From the cisterns, it is stored or pumped into two 25,000-gallon holding tanks. The central irrigation system collects rainwater from 17,000 square feet of roof. For each inch of rainwater, the system collects 10,000 gallons of water.

"It works very well," Heffington said. "We needed a system that wouldn't

harm the aquifer yet meet our water requirements and this one really works."

Like everything else at LBJWC, the cisterns not only look like they belong here, they are also functional.

The outer covering of sandstone fits with the early-European or Spanish design of the center's buildings. Designers wanted to keep the motif in line with the early settlers of the hill country. Spanish mission styling from the mid-1500s, German style structures from the mid-1800s and ranch-style buildings are in evidence. From the aqueduct which greets visitors near the main entrance to the courtyard and theme gardens, the structures are all constructed with native materials.

"We brought in a lot but the whole concept was sort of the building envelope," Heffington said. "If we could have brought the buildings in by helicopter and dropped them in, we would have done it that way.

"We slowed down the (building) process. The building was done in 18 months. It probably could have been done in 14 if we hadn't been so stringent on what we would and would not allow the builders to do. We did preserve a tremendous amount of the natural habitat."

Environmentally friendly options were utilized whenever possible. For example, instead of a concrete or asphalt fire lane, the LBJWC's fire lane is an avenue consisting of buffalo grass.

"We did it backwards," Heffington said. "Most people bring in architects, put buildings here, buildings there, then bring in landscapers and they try to clean up the mess and plant things around the edges and try to make things look nice.

"What we did was the very opposite. We brought in our site designer and our landscape people first. Of course, they worked very seriously to try to site where the buildings should be and they worked with the architects and the staff to develop an overall comprehensive plan of how this thing should work. They did a lot of traveling, looking at what does and does not work at botanical gardens, nature centers and natural history museums across the country."

Very little was disturbed during the building process.

"The few species that were disturbed, we're trying to put back in and enhance it," Heffington said. "We have between 415 and 500 species of plants on site and most of them were here or

nearby when we moved here."

The result was a natural wonder. At any time of the year several species are in bloom and in late February visitors are immediately greeted with the fragrant aroma of laurel in bloom. Bluebonnets are beginning to burst from their buds and in April, when most of the center's wildflowers are in bloom, the rainbow of colors is a breathtaking sight and one that makes that month the center's busiest time of the year.

"A lot of people have the misconception that native flowers aren't as colorful as the non-native species," Alholm says. "When they come here, the usual reaction is one of surprise."

That is part of the education process the center seeks to disseminate. Stroll the bark-mulched lined Meadow Path and you will follow a meandering trail lined by sugar hackberry, ten-petal anemone, lyre-leaf sage and King Ranch bluestem.

The red berries of yaupon, the interesting patterns of Texas persimmon and Texas prickly pear cactus and elbow bush are but a few to be found. Hundreds more, including Maximilian sunflower, ashe juniper, tasajillo, cedar, bigtooth maple, spring herald and mustang grape can be found along the Forest Trail. There are plenty of species of trees, from post oak to pecan as well.

The quarter-mile paths wind around the acreage, past a limestone cave, woodlands, arbor of oaks and a wildflower meadow before returning to the courtyard and theme gardens. The cave had to be emptied of eight truckloads of garbage left by generations of settlers, who used the cave as a dumping ground.

"We found debris that had to have

Wildflower Center Photo

There are programs, exhibits and gardens just for children.

been in there for decades," Alholm said.

The Seed Court was one of the first areas utilized as some 70,000 seedlings grown at the original site were planted. The gardens of the Seed Court are designed to provide a transition between the formal landscaping of the courtyard and the national landscaping of the Meditation Garden, a work still in progress.

Among the most popular and educational areas of the center are the 23 theme gardens. These square plots are separated by flagstone walkways showing the variety, uses and adaptations of native plants. This area also features comparison gardens, displaying native and non-native plants and wildflowers in a yard setting. This gives visitors ideas on how they might use wildflowers in their own yards.

"Too often people believe native means wild or unkempt," Alholm said. "These gardens show that that doesn't have to be the case."

One of the beds is for buffalo grass. Another, which is placed in full sun, is a xeric bed for cacti and wildflowers that require full sun. The theme gardens dis-

play plants and wildflowers native to Central Texas in a setting to give visitors an idea of how to use these native plants.

"You change your perspective by seeing," Heffington said. "It's an art to see what's part of your natural environment and paying attention to what your flora and fauna is. It's the interaction with all the plants and animals."

Wild turkeys have been spotted on the grounds and numerous native birds are visible year-round. By showing the beauty and value of using native plants and how they work with the environment, the center hopes to educate the public and corporate landscapers in that regard. Thus far the process is working at the grass-roots level.

"Not as many (corporations) as we'd like to are (using the center's methods)," Heffington said. "A few are, but mostly it's the individual gardener, landscaper or homeowner and it's not utterly pervasive nationwide by any stretch. But there is certainly an incredible interest right now and it is growing.

"Since we opened we've had tremendous foot traffic of officials from other museums and botanical gardens and we're one of the few botanical gardens in the country that has a facility just for children."

The center remains non-profit and self-funded. Part of the funds have been raised by after-hours events such as weddings, business meetings, class reunions, etc.

Conferences for department of transportation personnel from various states give the center's staff opportunities to educate decision-makers on the benefits of wildflowers as well as a first-hand look at wildflower benefits.

"Right now there's a much bigger emphasis on education than there is on research," Heffington said. "We will always have our research component and we try to make our facility available for researchers."

Johnson is pleased.

"Our goal was to become a resource, a clearing house of information to encourage the use of native wildflowers, grasses, shrubs, vines and trees, where appropriate, in the public and private landscapes of North America," she said. "Along the way, we hoped to influence the increased use of indigenous plants for two very good reasons: economic savings through decreased mowing, lower water requirements, reduced application of fertilizers, decreased use of pesticides, and dear to my heart, the aesthetic value of wildflowers bringing beauty, regionalism and seasonal color.

"Tongue in cheek, someone once wrote that I had done what every politician wishes he could do: I had associated myself with an issue as close to home as inflation, as popular as a tax cut and as necessary as national security."

That belief remains alive and well today. The growth of both the center and the membership has convinced Johnson she is on the right track today just as she was in 1982.

"This tells us ours is a cause whose time has come and which claims a rightful place in the whole mosaic of environmental concerns," she said. "May the seeds we have planted continue to grow." ❂

Want to Go There? Here's How

The Lady Bird Wildflower Center is located at 4801 La Crosse Avenue in Austin. From downtown Austin, go south on I-35 to the Slaughter Lane exit, drive west 5.8 miles to Loop 1 (Mopac), turn south to La Crosse Avenue, then turn east into the center.

LBJWC is closed on Mon. Hours:

Main Grounds: Tues. through Sun., 9 a.m.–5:30 p.m.

Visitors Gallery: Tues. through Sat., 9 a.m.–4 p.m.; Sun., 1–4 p.m.

Wild Ideas: The Store: Tues. through Sat., 9 a.m.–5:30 p.m.; Sun., 1–4 p.m.

Wildflower Cafe: Tues. through Sun., 10 a.m.–4 p.m. Sun., 11 a.m.–4 p.m.

Admission: $3.50 for adults, $2 for students and senior citizens and $1 for children 18 months to 5 years.

Call the registrar's office (512-292-4200) for group rates and reservations for guided tours.

Please note the LBJWC is smoke-free. Picnic areas are available. No pets or alcoholic beverages are allowed. Memberships. beginning at $25, includes free admission to the gardens, a 10 percent discount at the Center's store and mail catalog, a subscription to Wildflower, among many other benefits.

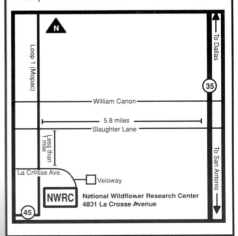

Skip Tradition – Go Wild with Your Home Garden

By PAUL COX
Acting Director
San Antonio Botanical Gardens

As we cruise along the Texas highways, it's easy to become enchanted with the beautiful wildflower displays. After all, these showy plants are hardy and they seem to thrive with minimal or no maintenance. It's many a homeowners' dream to have an attractive landscape that doesn't require a lot of attention. Native plants require less water, fertilizers, pesticides and other related garden chemicals.

But if you decide to start a wildflower garden at home, don't expect it to be a walk in the park — forgive the pun.

Some of the most practical lessons the wildflower novice must learn are patience, planning and foresight. It's a common impulse when viewing a patch of wildflowers to think, "I want that in my yard." What many don't realize is that — with a few exceptions — most wildflowers require a fairly long growing season to fill out properly.

The bluebonnet, for instance, started out as seeds which germinated the year before in late summer or early fall. During the winter, the plant sends out roots, forming rosette leaves and gathering strength for their spring thrust. Therefore, to obtain a decent display, it's necessary to plant the seeds or transplant according to the natural life-cycle.

Planting the right plant in the wrong location is another common mistake. Although many wildflowers prefer well-drained sites, there are wildflowers for almost any area. There are species for seasonally wet spots as well as those for permanently moist, boggy conditions, swampy or downright aquatic.

The idea here is to know your plant. Does it require sun or shade? How tall will it get? How much moisture does it require? These are questions that have to be answered for a successful wildflower garden.

Pre-packed wildflower seed mixes are available. These are composed of culturally compatible species. Be sure and read the package as most of these mixes are designed specifically for particular regions.

A word of warning here. Some wildflowers can be very aggressive and eventually take over an area. Mexican hat is one of these. It's as robust and rugged as it is pretty. Left alone, it will soon dominate an area.

The first criteria is knowing what you want. A frequent mistake is getting a quantity of mixed wildflower seeds and planting them not knowing what to expect.

The result is often disappointing. Many people are surprised by a somewhat "weedy" looking patch. Applied to an entire front yard, the response can

San Antonio Botanical Center Photo

Some wildflowers, such as Mexican hats, can be very aggressive. If left alone they will eventually take over an area.

be both frustrating and a problem. Neighborhood associations often take a dim view of yards totally committed to wildflowers. People with finely manicured yards can become outraged by an adjacent lot they view as unsightly.

Wildflower landscapes for the most part don't look like St. Augustine or any of the more traditional lawns. Even rational neighbors can lose their cool when it comes to an "untidy" lot.

Depending upon the individual relationship, the usual progression goes something like this: First the neighbors begin to cajole, then criticize.

Eventually they pretend to just ignore it, but secretly they have already called the authorities to complain about your unruly yard, no doubt which attracts rats, mice and other unsavory characters. Code Compliance Depart-

ments are notoriously inflexible and tenacious.

Some are becoming more enlightened and more receptive to ideas like "wildscaping." but don't count on it.

A few homeowners have gone to court and won. Their defense was to either produce receipts showing that their plants were intentionally planted and maintained, or point out the educational value of their plants by labeling various species.

But unless you are the type of person who just likes to fight the system, it is unwise to convert the entire yard into a mixture of different wildflowers. A more moderate approach would be to devote portions of the yard, such as edges or difficult spots, to the less traditional landscape.

Establishing a wildflower garden

can be therapeutic and fun for the whole family. It is relatively easy and if properly done can provide a long-lasting reward. The steps to follow are fairly simple and begin with some basics:

Bed Preparation

Simply scattering seed over an unprepared seed bed amounts to nothing more than feeding the birds. Most of our full-sun wildflowers are pioneer species. That is, they usually are the first to colonize areas of disturbed soils. Therefore, for best results, we need to try and duplicate natural conditions.

The first order is to create a favorable seed bed. Existing ground covers must be eliminated. This is best accomplished with the use of a contact herbicide such as *Roundup*. DO NOT USE A SOIL STERILANT.

These chemicals are what the name implies. A soil sterilizer will kill all plant life, not only in the target area, but often in the soil affecting trees and shrubs some distance from the initial application as well.

The degree and time it takes to travel in the soil depends on soil texture and moisture. Chemicals travel farther and faster in sandy soils, slower and less distance in heavy clays.

Accidentally using a soil sterilizing chemical, or even some stronger herbicides designated for brush control, can be a costly mistake. The treated soil must be removed or a bed built up to such a degree that desirable plant roots will never come into contact with the contaminated soil below. Reading the label of any garden chemical before using it cannot be over-emphasized.

San Antonio Botanical Center Photo

Milkweed

Failure to follow the printed directions can be disastrous, not only by damaging trees and shrubs on your property, but also your neighbor's. The liability of injuring plant material on the lot next door is worthy of serious consideration.

Once the target area is identified, outline it with a hose or piece of rope. Before applying the herbicide, read and follow the instructions printed on the container. Use the recommended formulations. The old adage. "If a little bit is good, then a lot must be better," is not appropriate when using garden chemicals.

Be aware of wind conditions as many nearby plants can be victims of "friendly fire" due to wind drift. It is recommended to mix an "indicator" with your herbicide. These are inert chemical markers, usually available in shades of green, that allow the applicator to see where they've sprayed the chemical.

Start in one corner and apply the herbicide with the same strategy as painting a floor. If you walk through a place that has been freshly sprayed, the chemical will stick to your shoes and spread to adjoining spots. Many homeowners have been surprised to later discover yellow or brown footsteps in their turf areas caused by walking through the area they've sprayed and then unknowingly traipsing into their own yard.

A follow-up application may be required 10 days to two weeks later to eliminate the stubborn spots.

Once the area has been purged of growing plants, it is necessary to remove the top cover so that the wildflower seed can be brought into contact with the bare mineral soil. This can be accomplished by raking or tilling. Vigorous use of a garden rake will remove the cover and scratch the soil sufficiently.

However, using the garden-rake technique is really only a half-hearted attempt on most soils and might result in a disappointing display. A more effective method is to use a rototiller. Many of our wildflowers enjoy an easy root run. Till the soil to a depth of one-to-three inches, then use a leaf rake to remove unwanted thatch. The bed is now ready for planting.

An alternative is to plant in raised beds. These only need to be built up about 6-to-12 inches and can be made from a variety of materials. Keep in mind that virtually all of our lawn grasses spread by runners. Therefore any gap in the bed border will provide an easy avenue for grass infiltration. A rock border should be mortared together to prevent a multitude of openings. Railroad ties and landscape timbers are probably the simplest and most cost effective. Ordinary garden soil will do for back-fill.

A good rule of thumb when planting the seeds is that they should be planted no deeper than the thickness of the width of the seed. The seeds can be broadcast over the prepared area by hand or using a fertilizer sprayer. Mix the seeds with sand for a more uniform distribution. Make several passes in one direction, then switch to several passes at right angles to your previous direction.

Thicker seeds such as bluebonnets need to be covered only slightly while minute seeds like Texas bluebell should be pressed into the soil. The best method for achieving uniform results is to use a roller over the area.

Another method is to use the flat side of a garden rake and gently drag it across the seeded area. This will lightly cover and impress the seeds but care must be taken not to go too deeply or the seeds will end up in uneven clumps with erratic germination.

Of course, you also can raise your own seedlings in containers and plant them when they are ready. This does offer the flexibility of arranging plants on a smaller scale utilizing color combinations, textures and heights.

Watering

Newly planted seeds must be watered for best results. A fine spray of water is best. Using the unbroken flow from a garden hose will wash the seeds around and result in erratic clumps. More native plants are killed from over-watering than by any other causes. Water again when the top one-half-to-one-inch layer of soil is dry.

Weeds

Weeds are basically plants that you don't like, generally determined by their location and behavior. Grasses can be the scourge of wildflower plantings. Winter grasses are especially detrimental to those wildflowers such as bluebonnets that over-winter as rosettes.

The fast-growing grasses quickly overgrow juvenile seedlings, choking and shading them out. There are selective herbicides that only affect grass and related species.

These chemicals must be applied with care if there are other desirable monocots present such as blue-eyed grass or members of the lily family. Dicot weeds can be either physically removed or, if they are more vigorous than the desired wildflowers, it is possible to herbicide them selectively.

Once the weeds have grown sufficiently taller than the wildflower seedlings, a wick applicator with an appropriate herbicide can be used. Pass the applicator over the area so that only the tops of the weeds come into contact. Be sure to use the same floor-painting application technique here.

Another herbicide technique for small areas is to wear rubber gloves

Herbicides must be applied with extra care around desirable monocots such as the rain lily.

with cotton gloves over them. Prepare an herbicide solution, dip you hands into the solution and wipe them on the intended victim. While this method is somewhat more labor intensive, it does have a certain personal satisfaction associated with it.

Physical removal of weed species by hoeing or pulling requires a basic knowledge of plant identification. The best results come from eliminating competitive weeds as early as possible. Remember the old Dutch proverb, "If you kill one weed before it sets seed, you've killed 10."

Some weeds such as sow thistle and the evil hedge parsley (torilis arvenis) can easily be identified at an early age. Weeds such as these have deep tap roots and need to be pulled or poisoned.

Removing the top by hoeing or by unsuccessful pulling attempts only aggravates the problem.

Thinning

Direct seeding often results in clumps of the desired wildflowers. These need to be thinned out for best results. Courage, faith and resolve are all needed to thin a tight group of desirable plants. Remove the smallest ones of the group.

If these runts are not removed, the entire cluster will become stunted and the display potential will be significantly reduced. Thinning in small areas is best accomplished by pinching off the unwanted. In larger areas, a hoe is best used when the plants get larger and those to be removed can easily be picked out.

Fertilizing

For the most part, native plants naturally live in an austere environment and don't require supplemental fertilization. Almost all of them will benefit from feeding but only a few can handle "the good life."

Bluebonnets for instance will produce prolific blooms with additional feeding, but many others can't tolerate coddling.

They tend to overgrow themselves often getting leggy and falling over. The results can be champion-sized plants with large sprawling vegetative stems and a few flowers clustered at the tips.

Woodland species like Jack-in-the-pulpit and meadow-rue prefer a richer, more organic soil. This holds true for the water-loving rose-mallows.

Problems

With the exception of over-watering or excessive fertilization, most native wildflowers suffer from very few problems. Problems often exist as perceived rather than realized. Milkweeds (asclepias) species often are infested with yellow melon aphids. Although the first aphids might look like a severe infestation, they seldom cause much damage to the plant. Like the milkweed plants attracted butterflies, the aphids are delectable to ladybugs.

Aristolochia species are the favorite food for the pipe-vine swallow tail butterfly larvae. These weird-looking fleshy caterpillars will often denude a plant. But the plant will rebound as if it were all part of the program. Indeed, plants and insects have evolved a coexistence over a long period of time. Natural predators and defense mechanisms form a balance that is millions of years old. Instead of interfering, try to observe and enjoy their interaction.

Flowering

The fulfillment of a plant existence, for all we know, is the production of seed to perpetuate the species. In annual species this is accomplished during the one year of growth. Once seeds have been formed and matured, the plant's task is done and it begins to wither and eventually die. To frustrate this process, it is possible to remove faded flowers and extend the formation of a plant's sexual organs, the flowers,

San Antonio Botanical Center Photo

***Winecups are rugged perennials that won't need re-seeding.
They should keep coming back no matter what you do.***

for as long as possible.

While this generally works for annual and perennial species, it is not reliable for biennials. Species of this nature usually form a basal rosette during the first year. During this time, they are developing sufficient energy for a big push the second year. The effort they have waited so long for is not easily frustrated. They rarely have enough strength left over to develop a second flower. So dead-heading the flower might only result in a weak second bloom at best.

The two most popular biennial species we grow in Texas are mullein and standing cypress (ipomopsis rubra).

Re-seeding

Constant dead-heading results in little if any seed production. Obviously to perpetuate the annual species such as phlox, coreopsis and bluebonnet, they must be allowed to produce seed. Removal of forming seed heads is, therefore, a strategic issue.

Rugged, reliable perennials such as cut-leaf daisy and wine-cups are not a concern as they will be back no matter what. Annuals or short-lived perennial species such as our native penstemons should probably be allowed to go to seed.

This often results in one of the pleasant surprises associated with wildflower gardening. That is to have our cultivated species pop up in some of the most unsuspected places such as crevices and border junctures.

Dead-heading can be a quick reward with a short-term goal. The major problem with allowing native plants to fulfill their seed cycle is that during the

San Antonio Botanical Center Photo

Annuals such as phlox must be allowed to produce seed.

time when the seeds are maturing, the plants often look "tacky," brown and withered. Without continued management, the wildflower garden will eventually tend towards the perennial members of its composition. Very few annual species can survive over the long haul without occasional bed renovation.

Seeds vs. Transplants

Sowing seeds is fairly easy and the primary preference of most gardeners. Transplants on the other hand are more expensive and labor intensive. Direct seeding, while requiring less effort, also offers the least reliable results. Germinating seeds are susceptible to fungal infections, pillbugs, snails, slugs

and watering extremes.

Transplants, on the other hand, offer a stronger plant that is already past the delicate state, so they are hardier. About the only way to kill them is by planting them too deep or over-watering.

One of the problems with transplants is availability. There are only a few native wildflower species that are commercially produced. These are phlox drummondii, bluebonnets and bluebells (eustoma grandiflora).

Another problem is stunting. Often when annuals are grown in containers too long, they get so root-bound they become stunted. A good rule of thumb when buying these plants in those two-inch, six-packs is, if they are already flowering, it is too late for a good display. That is why they are often "on sale."

Perennial wildflowers are usually available in larger containers and even if severely root-bound, most plants will eventually grow out of it.

One way to expedite this is, prior to planting, spread the roots out so they're no longer growing in the same configuration as the container. This seems brutal at the time but is necessary for the plant's future health.

One good thing about perennial species is that some of them can be propagated by divisions. These can be separated at just about any time of the year other than when in full bloom as long as a good root ball is included.

Growing wildflowers really doesn't take that much effort. In the long run, it sure beats watering, fertilizing and mowing the lawn. So think outside the lines, throw tradition to the wind and go wild with your garden. ✸

LEAF AND FLOWER FORMS

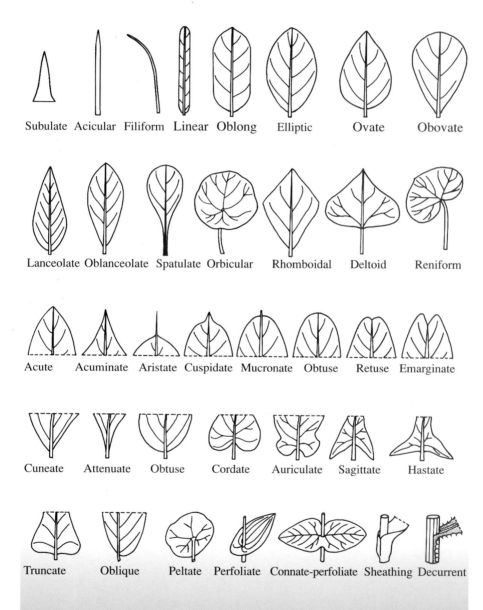

Subulate Acicular Filiform Linear Oblong Elliptic Ovate Obovate

Lanceolate Oblanceolate Spatulate Orbicular Rhomboidal Deltoid Reniform

Acute Acuminate Aristate Cuspidate Mucronate Obtuse Retuse Emarginate

Cuneate Attenuate Obtuse Cordate Auriculate Sagittate Hastate

Truncate Oblique Peltate Perfoliate Connate-perfoliate Sheathing Decurrent

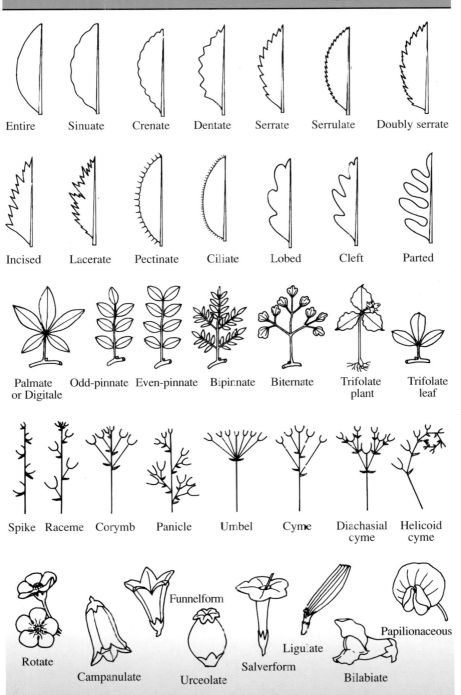

Entire Sinuate Crenate Dentate Serrate Serrulate Doubly serrate

Incised Lacerate Pectinate Ciliate Lobed Cleft Parted

Palmate or Digitale Odd-pinnate Even-pinnate Bipinnate Biternate Trifolate plant Trifolate leaf

Spike Raceme Corymb Panicle Umbel Cyme Diachasial cyme Helicoid cyme

Rotate Campanulate Funnelform Urceolate Salverform Ligulate Bilabiate Papilionaceous

DECORATING TEXAS:
HOW TxDOT GOT INTO THE WILDFLOWER BUSINESS

By KERRY BLACKMON
Texas Department of Transportation

When spring arrives in Texas, the state becomes a festival of colors. Wildflowers blanket the roadside in a rainbow carpet as the Texas bluebonnet and all of its vivid companions emerge from the winter of hibernation. Even the most tedious drive becomes a fascinating journey.

As most Texans know, this often dazzling array of wildflowers which spreads to every corner of the state is no accident. But many people don't know how far back the state's commitment to landscaping goes.

Most attribute the vast program of Texas wildflowers to Lady Bird Johnson, the former First Lady whose love of and tremendous contributions to nature has merited international recognition. But the story behind our Texas wildflower heritage began long before the Johnsons lived in the White House.

Early state-wide efforts to wrap our roadways in wildflowers was initiated by the State Department of Highways, which was created in 1917. The department currently is known as the Texas

Wildflower mix on U.S. 281 North of Marble Falls.

Department of Transportation or TxDOT.

Texas was one of the last (45th) states in the U.S. to set up a highway department. Despite this slow start, Texas was quick to address highway beautification and environmental issues. The advancement in wildflower awareness during the early stages of highway construction led to a beautification heritage that began in 1929 and to preservation and maintenance practices that encouraged the establishment of roadside wildflowers and natural landscapes.

The state's first landscape architect, Dutchman Jac Gubbels, was hired by the department in 1932 to promote the practical use and attractiveness of wildflowers and native plants to highway personnel and the public. The early highway engineers recognized that wildflowers not only put on quite a show in the spring and early summer, but helped prevent soil erosion.

Encouraged by this campaign, the department set up a program in 1933 to build roadside parks where travelers could relax and enjoy the scenery. Subsequently, more than 800 picnic areas were constructed around the state.

By 1934, plans were implemented to create the first official wildflower program for the department. New policies delayed mowing the right-of-ways until the wildflowers' blooming season was over. This practice is in its 64th year and is still a significant part of the wildflower management process.

As construction began on the first highways, it became apparent that the process required a radical manipulation of the natural grade. Sometimes these highways crossed

Bluebonnets on Loop 360 in Austin.

TxDOT Photo

meadows or pastures, where wildflowers flourished. Since many species of wildflowers thrive in poor, disturbed soils where competition from other plants is limited, often the first vegetation to emerge on these bare roadsides were wildflowers.

No commercially harvested seeds were available in the 1930s, so alternate methods of wildflower distribution were established. One of these methods included locating a prominent growth of wildflowers that was in or near the path of the new highway.

With permission of the land owner, the wildflower stalks would be cut with a sickle mower after the peak blooming period and before the seeds had dropped. The "wildflower hay" would be gathered, transported and then scattered along the bare roadsides of the new highway. This helped hold the soil in place while allowing the seeds contained in the "hay" to be deposited onto the soil. This worked well, since the wildflower seeds only need to come in contact with the soil to germinate.

Enough seed would remain at the original locations to continue generating an abundance of blooms. Usually, highway construction took place after the seeds had already dropped. In this procedure, a blade would pass under the wildflowers, removing a thin layer of soil containing the seeds. The soil was stockpiled until the construction was complete and then spread on the exposed roadside.

These methods and any variations were used until commercially harvested seed was available. Reports indicate that by 1940, an estimated 500,000

pounds of wildflower seed had been distributed along the highways, utilizing these methods. The transplanting of trees and shrubs, in association with highway construction, also became a common practice by the department.

By 1936, more than 200,000 trees and 500,000 shrubs were transplanted along state highways. These methods are still used, although commercial seed sources and technology are making it economically feasible to sow the seed by modern methods such as hydroseeding, broadcast seeding or drill seeding.

In 1965, President Johnson promoted highway landscaping projects through the Highway Beautification Act. Through this effort, more than 100 comfort stations were provided along Texas highways. This significant accomplishment, along with Ms. Johnson's outstanding contribution in promoting wildflowers, supported the department's commitment to remain focused on highway beautification.

Her inspiring motto: "Where flowers bloom, so does hope," has encouraged many to join her in the creation of the Lady Bird Johnson Wildflower Center in Austin.

TxDOT continues the advancement of highway beautification through progressive design and modern roadside management techniques. The department regularly explores practices that reduce competitive vegetation and enhance wildflower production.

New programs have emerged within the department that underscore their dedication to attractive roadsides. Since 1985, the Texas Highway Commission has obligated state construction funds in excess of $45 million in support of various statewide landscape programs.

The Landscape Construction Program was created to establish a systematic funding source to encourage landscape improvement throughout the highway system. It is generally based upon one percent of the total construction costs of highway construction of the previous fiscal year. The Landscape Cost Sharing Program provides an opportunity to encourage joint beautification of our state highway system. County and city governments may participate in the development of highway landscaped projects for their benefit.

Another program that attracts city participation is through the Landscape Incentive Awards Program. This program was developed in cooperation with Keep Texas Beautiful Inc., a part of the Keep America Beautiful system which advances quality of life, anti-litter and beautification issues.

Cities compete in nine population categories and every year the state allocates funds to develop landscape projects for the nine winning cities. Winning cities cooperate with TxDOT by suggesting sites and design concepts.

TxDOT also is responsible for one of the most outstanding and successful anti-litter campaigns in American. "Don't Mess With Texas" has become one of the most recognizable phrases in our state.

As the blooms have spread along our roadsides, a new wildflower industry has emerged in Texas. Visitors and tourists now flock to Texas to enjoy the springtime display. Tourism has increased as well as the demand for

TxDOT Photo

Bluebells on Lake Travis.

commercially grown seed.

Through it all, TxDOT remains determined to build safe, efficient, and beautiful highways. TxDOT currently maintains more than 77,000 miles of highway and manages more than 1,320,000 acres of right-of-way.

These roadsides are the habitat of more than 900 species of animals and approximately 5,500 species of plants which includes more than 2,000 species of wildflowers.

In an ongoing effort to keep the highway right-of-way in bloom, the Department now purchases and plants approximately 60,000 pounds of wildflower seed annually.

Every spring, TxDOT highway crews watch for the best wildflower hot-spot locations.

They share this information with the public through a Statewide Information Hotline (1-800-452-9292). For the Austin District, including the hill country, that number is 512-832-7125. ●

NATIVE PLANT SOCIETY GROWING LIKE WILDFLOWERS

By JIM MOLONY

Carroll Abbott didn't live long enough to see the Native Plant Society of Texas he formed grow into the thriving organization it has become today but the former newspaperman and press secretary for President Lyndon Johnson would probably be proud of his legacy.

"Carroll Abbott started this in 1984," Native Plant Society of Texas president Peter Loos said. "After he got out of the writing business he pursued his love of wildflowers, he sold seeds and tried to get the word out about wildflowers."

Abbott annually attended the Wildflower Days celebrations each spring, such as the one at Texas Woman's University in Denton, and through his travels he learned other states, like California, had organizations devoted to native plants. Abbott saw no reason a regional plant organization couldn't be formed in the Lone Star State.

In 1984, Abbott and a few friends with a common love of native plants formed the Native Plant Society of Texas.

Abbott passed away in Kerrville shortly after the society's formation but the organization continued to grow with each season.

"Around 1986 we divided the organization into six regions," Loos said. "Then it reached a point where those were getting too big so we started creating individual chapters."

Hill Country scene.

Today the Native Plant Society of Texas numbers approximately 1,800 members and 30 chapters throughout the state.

The group holds its annual meeting the third weekend of October. For the last five years the meeting has been held in a different vegetative region of the state.

"Originally our focus was the promotion of preservation, conversation and research and since then we've added utitlization," Loos said.

"We try to achieve these goals through education, outreach and example."

The group's official publication, "The Native Plant Society of Texas News" is published six times annually. Education is one of the main "pushes" the organization is heavily involved with presently.

The group does not simply enjoy native plants and wildflowers but seeks to educate the general public regarding the numerous advantages, both economic and environmental, of using native plants and wildflowers.

"We communicate with a lot of range management associations, more than we have in the past and the number is growing," Loos said.

"We don't care if they're public, private or whatever. The more people we can educate the better off we'll all be."

The society has been in discussions with officials from the Texas Department of Transportation regarding highway beautification and environmentally friendly roadside projects and helped the TxDOT establish guidelines for plant use.

One of the society's functions is to monitor the work projects and ensure the guidelines are being followed, although members are instructed to be informative and never confrontational if they witness a guideline that is not being followed.

Research remains a main aspect of the group's function. By continuing to discover more uses, benefits and knowledge regarding native plants and disseminating that information to as wide an audience as possible the society hopes to continue to help the people and the environment.

The gardens the society plants in communities around the state are area specific as well as educational.

"If I'm going to do one in Conroe you can be sure every plant used in that garden will be found within a 50-mile radius of the site," Loos said.

Using vegetation indigenous to the area has economic benefits as well as environmental advantages.

"We teach people that it is cheaper to use a plant that is native to the area and thus obviously is well adapted to the area, rather than something that is non-native," Loos said.

"Since by definition they have to be imported, non-native plants not only cost more, in many cases they aren't as adaptable to the area and require more care, which contributes both to time and money costs."

The cost savings is a major aspect of the society's appeal to the Texas Department of Transportation, but the bottom line advantages are also appealing to more and more homeowners and small businesses wishing to improve their grounds without gouging their pocketbooks.

"Once people are educated about native plants they tend to reach these conclusions," Loos said. "Our goal is to educate them while continuing our research."

Group members share insights and research information and work together to plan the best garden projects possible for specific areas of Texas. Some specialize in one region or another. The annual meetings are a time when members exchange information and plan the coming year.

The Native Plant Society of Texas also works extensively with numerous other conservation organizations, such as the Prairie Preservation Society, in a concerted effort to protect the environment through shared research and a mutual respect for natural resources.

"The Austin chapter, for example, could be busy year-round with garden projects," Loos said. "The Beaumont chapter recently applied for a grant for a school garden.

"We seem to be growing pretty good." Abbott would be pleased. ✳

Native Plant Society of Texas

Local chapter contacts and meeting times
(Listings can change. Call to confirm.)

Abilene — Ronald Schulze, Rt. 1, Box 399B, Abilene 79601. 915-548-2264

Amarillo —Third Tuesday February–October; Regina McMullan, 520 W. 5th, Amarillo 79101. 806-374-8866

Austin — Fourth Tuesday of every month, 7 p.m. LCRA Headquarters, 3701 Lake Austin Blvd. Ginger Hudson-Maffei, 11702 Tedford, Austin 78753. 512-836-4751

Bandera — Second Thursday, 7 p.m., St. Christopher's Church Bandera Doris Uhl, NPSOT P.O. Box 2333, Bandera 78003-9510

Beaumont — First Thursday, 7 p.m. Ridgewood Church of Christ; Sharon Odegar, 6 Stradford Drive, Orange 77632. 409-886-1877

Belton (Tonkawa) — Last weekend of the month, varying by speaker schedules; Marie Kline, 134 Woodland Trail, Belton 76513. 817-780-1715

Big Bend Area (Trans Pecos) — John Mac Carpenter, P.O. Drawer 430, Ft. Stockton 79735. 915-336-3826

Collin County — First Tuesday 7:30 p.m., Heard Museum, Fm 1378 in McKinney; Betsy Farris, 4205 Tynes Drive, Garland 75402. 972-494-2241

Columbus — Ann Lindemann, P.O. Box 218, Industry 78944. 409-357-2772

Corpus Christi (South Texas) — James Gill, 2810 Airline, Corpus Christi 78414. 512-992-9647

Dallas — Third Thursday of every other month, 7 p.m. Walnut Hill Recreation Center, 10011 Midway Rd. in Dallas; Hannah Larson, 1020 N. Cedar Hill 75104. 972-291-7545

Denton — Fourth Thursday, 6:30 p.m. Ben E. Keith Co. Hospitality Room, 2801 I-35E North; Lou Kraft, 1933 Laurelwood, Denton 76201. 817-923-4189

Fort Worth — First Thursday of every month, 7 p.m. at Ft. Worth Botanic Garden; Jim Leavy, 4115 Bellaire Dr. S., Ft. Worth 76109. 817-923-4189

Fredericksburg — Last Tuesday of every month, 7 p.m., Gillespie Co. Ag Building; Bill Lindeman, 884 Loudon Road, Fredericksburg 78624. 210-977-8917

Georgetown — Monthly at Georgetown Library; Armaund Hufault, 9531 FM 1105, Jarrell 76537. 512-746-5006

Houston — Third Thursday, 7 p.m. Houston Arboretum, 4501 Woodway Drive; Glenn Olsen, P.O. Box 721356, Houston 77272. 281-495-8144

Kerrville — First Tuesday 2 p.m.; C.R. (Bobby) Crabb, 108 Friar Tuck, Kerrville 78028. 210-257-7265

Lubbock (South Plains) — Roger Gras, 5108 55th Street, Lubbock 79414. 806-799-0464

Mercer Arboretum (Conroe) — Second Sunday bimonthly; 2 p.m.; Greg Wieland, 1700 Seaspray Ct. #2008, Houston 77008. 713-863-9582; 713-443-8731

Midland — Third Tuesday of every month, 7 p.m., Sibley Learning Center 1300 E. Wadley; Andra K. Chamberlin, 1710 WCR 130, Midland 79706. 915-687-2961

Navasota Valley (Groesbeck-Mexia) — Last Sunday of Feb., May, Aug. and Nov. at 3 p.m.; Francis Bates, Route 3, Box 27 Groesbeck 76642. 817-729-3307

Northeast Texas (Longview) — Third Thursday, 7 p.m. St. Mary's Catholic Church Parish Hall, 2108 Ridgewood, Longview; Logan Damewood, 3802 Holly Ridge Drive, Longview 75604. 903-757-2074

San Angelo (Concho Valley) — Last Tuesday, 7 p.m. Boatmans Bank 2302 Pullium St.; John Begnaud, 133 W. Beauregard, San Angelo 76903. 915-659-6528

San Antonio — Fourth Tuesday, 7 p.m., Lions Club Field House; Edward Schweninger, 2809 Old Rand Road, San Antonio 78217. 210-828-5956; 210-220-2139

San Marcos — Brad Smith, 23 Shady Grove, Wimberley 78676. 512-847-3342

Tyler — First Tuesday 7 p.m., UT Tyler — call contact for room number; Garry McDonald, 903-834-6191 (work); 903-854-2361 (home); email address: g-mcdonald@tamu.edu

Waco (Brazos Valley) — Last Monday, Li'l Greenhouse Nursery, Hewitt; Bob Chapman, 441 Lindenwood W., Hewitt 76643. 817-666-7046

Wichita Falls — (forming) Nila Dowlearn, 5314 SW Parkway, Wichita Falls 76310. 817-696-3082

Want to Join?

The Native Plant Society of Texas' state office address is:

Native Plant Society of Texas
Bank One Building
1111 N. Interstate Hwy 35
Suite 112
Round Rock, Texas 78664

Or: Box 891 Georgetown, 78627
The phone number for the state office is: **(512) 238-0695**.

TEXAS WILDFLOWER REGIONS

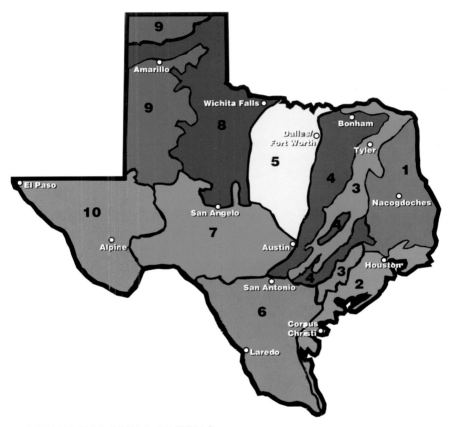

VEGETATIONAL AREAS OF TEXAS

1. Pineywoods
2. Gulf Prairies and Marshes
3. Post Oak Savannah
4. Blackland Prairies
5. Cross Timbers and Prairies
6. South Texas Plains
7. Edwards Plateau
8. Rolling Plains
9. High Plains
10. Trans-Pecos, Mountains and Basins

100
OF THE STATE'S
MOST POPULAR
WILDFLOWERS

LBJ Wildflower Center Photo

Antelope-horns
Asclepias asperula

Description — This perennial grows one-to-two-feet tall. Its spreading streams form dense clumps. Its stems are densely covered with small hairs.

Flower — The flowers are grouped into a ball-shaped head that is three-to-four inches across. Flowers grow at the end of each stem. Inside the partially divided petals is a crown, out of which five white stamens with large ball-like anthers.

Leaves — Leaves range from four-to-eight inches long. They are narrow and grouped irregularly.

Requirements — Prefers full sun and well-drained soil.

Habitat — Regions 4, 5, 6, 7, 8, 9, 10.

Bloom period — March through May.

Notes — Plant is also known as the green-flowered milkweed. ❁

LBJ Wildflower Center Photo

Basket Flower
Centaurea americana

Description — Plant stands three-to-six feet tall and forms dense colonies, covered with three-inch flower heads ranging in color from pink or rose to darker lavender. The stems are thick and upright. They are ridged and branched in the upper portions.

Flower — All the flowers are tubular, although they do not appear so. Heads, containing only disk flowers, are divided into five long, narrow lobes, all looking like stamens. The outer florets are much longer and darker than the center ones.

Leaves — Lance-like shaped leaves are alternate and stalkless.

Requirements — Prefers open fields and woodland edges.

Habitat — Regions 1, 2, 3, 4, 5, 6, 7, 8, 10.

Bloom period — May though August.

Notes — Before the flower is open, it resembles an old-fashioned shaving brush. ❁

San Antonio Botanical Center Photo

Beard Tongue
Penstemon baccharifolius

Description — Shrubby perennial to about one-and-a-half feet tall.

Flower — Tubular one-inch red flowers.

Leaves — Leaves are opposite, rarely in whorls of three.

Requirements — Prefers full sun.

Habitat — Regions 7, 10.

Bloom period — June through September.

Notes — Plant is excellent for drought resistance in well-drained locations. ❁

Big Bend Penstemon
Penstemon harvardii

Description — Short-lived perennial that grows three-to-five feet tall with gray-green foliage.

Flower — Red tubular flowers that grow an inch or so long.

Leaves — Elliptic to oblong and entire, they are leathery in appearance.

Requirements — Prefer full sun but might not persist in hot, dry locations.

Habitat — Regions 7, 8, 9, 10.

Bloom period — March through October.

Notes — Easy to grow from seed. It has a long blooming period and attracts hummingbirds. ❀

San Antonio Botanical Center Photo

San Antonio Botanical Center Photo

Blood Flower
Asclepias curassavica

Description — Fast-growing annual reaches two-to-three feet tall.

Flower — Bright flowers are crimson, rarely yellow or white. Lobes are three-eighths-of-an-inch. The hoods are orange.

Leaves — Leaves are opposite up to five inches long and some-what whorled.

Requirements — Prefers full sun with adequate moisture.

Habitat — Region 6.

Bloom period — April through August.

Notes — Yellow melon aphids, which attract ladybugs, frequently appear on the plant but don't cause any appreciable damage. ●

LBJ Wildflower Center Photo

Blue-eyed Grass
Sisyrinchium sagittiferum

Description — Plant grows eight-to-12 inches tall in clumps on thread-like stems.

Flower — Wide-open usually yellow-centered flowers close in the afternoon. Flowers are bluish to purple, occasionally white with six sepals one-half-to-three-quarters-of-an-inch across.

Leaves — Narrow grass-like leaves four-to-six inches long.

Requirements — Prefers sandy soil.

Habitat — Found in open woods and grassy areas. Regions 1, 2.

Bloom period — March through April.

Notes — There are many similar species in various parts of Texas with the greatest diversity found in sandy woods along the Gulf Coast of Southeast Texas. Characteristics separating the species are very fine. ❁

LBJ Wildflower Center Photo

Bluebells
Eustoma grandiflorum

Description — An upright, smooth, usually short-lived perennial that grows up to 28 inches.

Flower — Large and purple, the flower is up to four inches across. It has five petals that are united at the base and deeply cupped. Flowers form terminal cluster on slender stalks.

Leaves —Up to three-and-an-eighth inches long and one-and-a-fourth inches wide, leaves are opposite and stalkless. Leaves are noticeably three-vein and clasp the stem at the base.

Requirements — Prefers a moist, sunny site.

Habitat — Regions 1, 2, 3, 4, 5, 6, 7, 8, 9, 10.

Bloom period — June through September.

Notes — One of our most attractive wildflowers. The cut flowers last for several days. ❀

Bluebonnet
Lupinus texensis

Description — Plant grows 15-to-24 inches tall. Flowers are densely arranged on a spike with a characteristic ice white terminal tip.

Flower — The dark blue bloom on the upper two-to-six inches of the stem has two lips with five petals. The upper petal has a white center that usually turns wine-red or purplish as it ages.

Leaves — Leaves usually consist of five leaflets with pointed tips, joined at one point on a long stem. Each leaflet forms a little bowl that holds one large drop of water when it rains, giving the plant a shimmering dia-mond-like effect.

LBJ Wildflower Center Photo

Requirements — Prefers well-drained soils of fields and roadsides, especially limestone hillsides of Central Texas.

Habitat — Regions 1, 2, 3, 4, 5, 6, 7.

Bloom period — March through May.

Notes — Adopted state flower of Texas in 1901. All five species in Texas were designated as the state flower in 1971. ✿

San Antonio Botanical Center Photo

Butterfly Weed
Asclepias tuberosa

Description — This strong, long-lived perennial from a deep tap root can reach two feet tall.

Flower — Bright orange flowers are concentrated in compact clusters at the top of the branching stems. The flowers produce a large amount of nectar which attracts butterflies throughout the growing season.

Leaves — Leaves are mostly alternate, one-and-a-half-to-two-and-a-fourth inches long and smooth on the edges.

Requirements — Requires well-drained sandy or gravel-like soil in full sun.

Habitat — Regions 1, 2, 3, 4, 5, 6, 7, 8, 9, 10.

Bloom period — April through December.

Notes — The leaves are poisonous to livestock. Plant is difficult to transplant. It might take up to two years to become established from seed. Once established, it is very dependable. ❂

San Antonio Botanical Center Photo

Cancer-weed
Salvia lyrata

Description — Strictly upright, hairy perennial, the plant reaches one-to-two feet high with an upright hairy stem. It is square in cross section and rises from a basal rosette of leaves.

Flower — Three-quarters-of-an-inch-to-one-and-a-quarter across, the blossom is lone, pale blue to violet with two lips.

Leaves — To eight inches long, the leaves are mostly in basal rosette, deeply three-lobed with a few simple leaves higher up on the stem and they are often purplish.

Requirements — Full sun or partial shade.

Habitat — Sandy or occasionally clay or gravely soils in meadows, clearings, lowlands, slopes and open woodlands. Regions 1, 2, 3, 5.

Bloom period — March through June.

Notes — It is a herbaceous perennial with violet, blue flower spikes that is said to spread quickly like cancer. Also known as lyre-leaf sage. ❀

San Antonio Botanical Contor Photo

Cardinal Flower
Lobelia cardinalis

Description — An upright perennial with a simple stern from a basal rosette, the plant can reach six feet tall, but is generally three-feet or less. It is usually unbranched, but occasionally branched below the main flower spike.

Flower — Beautiful deep red flowers are about an inch or so long. The flowers are two-lipped. The upper lip is deeply two-lobed. The lower lip is three-lobed. The five stamens are united into a slender tube. There are numerous flowers in a showy spike.

Leaves — Leaves are alternate and thin. Irregularly at the base and sharply toothed, the leaves reach two-to-eight inches.

Requirements — Prefers moist, shady or partial sun locations and rich soil.

Habitat — Regions 1, 2, 3, 4, 5, 6, 7, 8, 9, 10.

Bloom period — May through December.

Notes — The plant contains alkaloids. Although the leaves were used medicinally and for smoking by the Indians, many deaths of early settlers were caused because of misuse or overdoses of plant derivatives. ❀

San Antonio Botanical Center Photo

Celestial Lily
Nemastylis geminiflora

Description — Perennial from a small bulb, the plant grows to about two inches tall.

Flower — Two to three in a spathe, the bloom reaches to two-and-a-half inches across. Filaments are separate or unite only at the base.

Leaves — To one foot long.

Requirements — Sun or shade, prefers prairies.

Habitat — Regions 1, 2, 3,4, 5, 6, 7, 8.

Bloom period — March through May.

Notes — Usually blue, it blooms in the early morning. ❁

San Antonio Botanical Center Photo

Chile Piquin
Capsicum annuum

Description — Long-lived and versatile, the much-branched plant grows from three-to-six feet tall.

Flower — The small white flower is about one-quarter-of-an-inch long. The flower is followed by decorative bright red fruit up to a half-inch long. It is solitary, rarely two at a node and five lobed.

Leaves — Leaves are lance-shaped and grow one-to-five inches. The leaves are alternate and simple.

Requirements — Grows in sun or shade.

Habitat — Regions 2, 4, 6, 7.

Bloom period — January through December.

Notes — Be sure to wash hands immediately after handling the edible, pungent peppers. ❁

San Antonio Botanical Center Photo

Chocolate Flower
Berlandiera lyrata

Description — A herbaceous short-lived perennial, the plant is erect, branched and grows to 20 inches.

Flower — The yellow, ray flowers with maroon centers smell like chocolate. The heads expand in the morning, but droop in the afternoon heat.

Leaves — The blades are oblong and grow to seven inches long. The leaves are coarse and are deeply pinnately lobed in the lower half.

Requirements — Prefers full sun in well-drained soils, especially rocky limestone.

Habitat — Regions 7, 8, 9, 10.

Bloom period — June through September.

Notes — When the yellow ray flowers drop, the green sepals underneath look like eyes. The plant is also known as the green-eyed lyre leaf. ❀

San Antonio Botanical Center Photo

Compass Plant
Silphium laciniatum

Description —
Robust perennial to six-feet tall that grows from a strong tap root.

Flower — Large clear yellow flowers three inches across.

Leaves —
Alternate and deeply pinnatified with some lower leaves reaching 20 inches long.

Requirements —
Thrives in good soil and full sunlight.

Habitat —
Regions 1, 2, 3, 4, 5, 6, 7.

Bloom period —
March through August.

Notes —
Established plants are difficult to transplant. Are useful for rear borders. ❁

San Antonio Botanical Center Photo

Coral Bean
Erythrina herbacea

Description — A perennial shrublet that freezes to the ground in most winters with stems reaching two-to-three feet tall. Can be taller in some southern areas.

Flower — The flowers are bright, red and tubular and grow to two inches long. They are followed by brown pods that split open to reveal hard, shiny scarlet seeds.

Leaves — Leaves are long-stalked and alternate and contain three leaflets.

Requirements — Prefers full sun to moderate shade.

Habitat — Regions 3, 6.

Bloom period — April through June.

Notes — The dried fruit is good for flower arrangements. Hummingbirds are attracted to this flower. ✿

I.B.J. Wildflower Center Photo

Coreopsis Tickseed
Coreopsis tinctoria

Description — Erect annual to three feet tall.

Flower — Bright yellow flowers are about one inch wide.

Leaves — Opposite, mostly once or twice divided that grows two-to-four inches.

Requirements — Prefers bright sunlight.

Habitat — Regions 1, 2, 3, 4, 5, 6, 7, 8, 9, 10.

Bloom period — March through July.

Notes — This is a very popular and prolific flower that is easy to grow from seed and is popularly known as the "golden wave." Also known as plains coreopsis. A dozen species of coreopsis thrive in Texas, many along bayous and river banks. Native Americans used root tea from coreopsis for treatment of diarrhea. Also used as a natural dye. ❀

Cupleaf Penstemon
Penstemon murrayanus

Description — A perennial that grows up to three-and-a-third feet tall, it has reddish stems.

Flower — The tubular red flower is over an inch long, opening into a five-petal-like lobe. Stamens extend beyond the flower, and the fifth stamen, which has no antler, is lightly bearded.

Leaves — Leaves are opposite. The upper ones are cup-shaped. Leaves are smooth on the edges and have a downy covering.

Requirements — Prefers sandy soils.

Habitat — Regions 1, 2, 3, 4, 7.

Bloom period — April through May.

Notes — This plant is also known as the scarlet penstemon. ❁

San Antonio Botanical Center Photo

San Antonio Botanical Center Photo

Devil's Claw
Proboscidea louisianica

Description — A glandular annual with upright or reclining stems that grow to three feet long.

Flower — Tubular flowers grow to one inch long.

Leaves — Nearly orbicular to ovate-cordate growing to a foot across.

Requirements — Plenty of sun.

Habitat — Regions 1, 2, 3, 4, 5, 7, 8, 10.

Bloom period — June through September.

Notes — The fruit of this odd-shaped flower is sometimes made into pickles.

The unusual fruit is also used in dried arrangements. Also known as unicorn plant. ❀

LBJ Wildflower Center Photo

Drummond's Phlox
Phlox drummondii

Description — Showy annual grows one-to-two feet tall.

Flower — One-quarter-to-one-half-inch wide, the plant features a wide range of colors from white, lavender, pink or purplish. The flower is sweetly fragrant, trumpet-shaped, five-lobed at rim, the lobes spreading flat, narrowed at base, wider and sharp-pointed at tip. Flowers are numerous with only a few opening at one time, forming terminal clusters.

Leaves — Leaves, to one-and-one-quarter inches long and one-quarter inch wide, are stalkless, opposite in lower portion of plant, becoming alternate and narrower in upper portion. The margins are entire.

Habitat — Regions 1, 2, 3, 4, 5, 6, 7, 8, 9.

Requirements — Prefers sandy or loamy soils in grasslands, prairies and open woodlands.

Bloom period — February through June.

Notes — This is popular ornamental used as a bedding plant. ❁

LBJ Wildflower Center Photo

Eastern Columbine
Aquilegia canadensis

Description — A perennial with airy sprays of flowers reaching almost two feet tall.

Flower — Flowers are almost two inches long and up to one-and-a-half inches across.

Leaves — Has basal leaves that reach to two inches.

Requirements — They do well in rock gardens and perennial borders. They do best in well drained soil.

Habitat — Regions 5, 7.

Bloom period — February through May.

Notes — Species readily hybridize so it is difficult to collect pure seeds when growing more than one type together. Also known as the wild columbine. ❂

LBJ Wildflower Center Photo

Engelmann Daisy
Engelmannia pinnatifida

Description — Common perennial of the plains and prairies that closely resembles the sunflower, but has the daisy characteristics of closing the flower heads at night and opening them in the bright sunlight. The rough hairy plants grow one-to-three feet tall

Flower — The plant is topped by broad clusters of showy yellow flower heads about one-and-a-half inches across. The eight-to-10 ray flowers are one-half-of-an-inch long and are indented at the tip.

Leaves — Leaves are alternate and are deeply cut. They reach three-to-six inches long. The upper leaves have coarse teeth.

Requirements — Prefers open areas.

Habitat — Regions 2, 3, 4, 5, 6, 7, 8, 9, 10.

Bloom period — March through July.

Notes — Also known as cut-leaved daisy. ❀

San Antonio Botanical Center Photo

Estafiate
Artemisia ludoviciana

Description — Perennial herb spreading from root sprouts to about 3-feet tall. Grown for its aromatic gray foliage.

Flower — White-tomentose beneath, almost glabrous above when old, with heads to one-eighth inch across, usually in rather dense panicles.

Leaves — Lanceolate to elliptic-lanceolate, up to four inches long, entire or merely lobed.

Requirements — Thrives even in poor, dry soil.

Habitat — Regions 1, 2, 3, 4, 5, 6, 7, 8, 9, 10.

Bloom period — March through August.

Notes — Benefits from periodic shearing. Popular ornamental in eastern states. Locally used medicinally for stomach disorders. ❀

False Dayflower
Commelinantia anomala

Description — Plant, can reach two feet tall is an annual with a blue flowers.

Flower — Blooms are showy and lavender-blue with one small and white.

Leaves — Upper leaves grow to eight inches long. The lower leaves are up to 12 inches. The inner perianth segments are very unequal.

Requirements — Prefers shade.

Habitat — Regions 2, 4, 5, 7.

Bloom period — May through August

Notes — The spathe below the flower produces a single drop of water or tear when squeezed. Also known as widow's tears. ✲

San Antonio Botanical Center Photo

San Antonio Botanical Center Photo

Flax
Linum rigidum

Description — This stiffly upright, thin and smooth annual grows 8-to-20 inches high. The stems are solitary. The upper portion of the plant is branched and the slender branches are prominently angled or winged.

Flower — One-and-a-half inches across, the yellow or copper-colored, flower has a dark reddish center with five petals that are cupped. The flower, which forms in terminal clusters, falls early.

Leaves — Leaves, from one-to-one-and-one-fourth inches long and about one-eighth-of-an inch wide, are alternate, stalkless, upright and rigid.

Requirements — Prefers full sun and a well-drained site with sandy, gravel-like, loose clay soil or chalky soils in prairies, pastures and edges of woodlands.

Habitat — Regions 2, 4, 5, 6, 7, 8, 9.

Bloom period — May through September.

Notes — Also known as stiff-stem flax. Flax plants are producers of fiber from which cloth, thread and cord are manufactured. Oil is also extracted from the seeds. The words linen, linseed and lingerie are all derived from the word linum. ✿

Foxglove
Penstemon cobaea

Description — Perennial that grows to almost three feet tall.

Flower — Tubular flowers can be white, pink or lavender with purple outlines.

Leaves — Opposite to three inches long with coarse teeth.

Requirements — Found in rocky, calcareous soils of prairies and roadsides. Prefers full sun and good drainage.

Habitat — Regions 2, 3, 4, 5, 6, 7, 8.

Bloom period — April through June.

Notes — Often seen in clumps along roadsides. Native Americans made a penstemon tea they used as a laxative. ❀

LBJ Wildflower Center Photo

San Antonio Botanical Center Photo

Fragrant Gailliardia
Gaillardia suavis

Description — A herbaceous perennial with fragrant flowers that look like buttons growing to about two feet tall. The plant is upright, slender and clumped. There are few to several stems.

Flower — Head is up to one-and-three-fourths inches across, very fragrant and solitary. The ray blooms are yellow to orange or red. They are very short and deeply three-lobed. The blooms soon fall off, leaving the disk, which is reddish-brown.

Leaves — Up to six inches long, the leaves are basal, thick and widest near the tip.

Requirements — Prefers full sun

Habitat — Heavy loams, clay, calcareous or sandy-calcareous soils of prairies, openings, old fields and pastures. Regions 2, 4, 5, 6, 7, 8, 9, 10

Bloom period — March through May.

Notes — Also known as button flower and pin cushion daisy. ❀

Gay-feather
Liatris species
compositae

Description — A simple mostly long and narrow to lance-shaped perennial that is entire and usually resin-dotted. The purple or pink spikes contrast with prairie grass. It is a stiffly upright to widely spreading plant that can reach 32 inches tall.

Flower — Heads are disc-shaped. The uppermost head of the flower always blooms first. Blooms are tubular, purple or rose-colored.

Leaves — Leaves are somewhat crowded and grow progressively smaller from the base of the plant.

Requirements — Prefers well-drained gravel or sand soils in full sun.

San Antonio Botanical Center Photo

Habitat — Regions: 1, 2, 3, 4, 5, 6, 7, 8, 9, 10.

Bloom period — July through October.

Notes — The gay-feather is also known as snakeroot and blazing stars. The corm has been used to treat rattlesnake bites as well as sore throats. ❁

San Antonio Botanical Center Photo

Giant Coneflower
Rudbeckia maxima

Description — Robust perennial with six-foot tall stalks of two-inch yellow flowers rising from a basal cluster of large bluish-gray green leaves. Stems are stiff and erect.

Flower — Ray petals are yellow and drooping, up to two inches long.

Leaves — Elliptic, up to 14 inches long, uppermost stem leaves are smaller, ovate, clasping; receptacle conic, becoming conic-cylindrical and two-to-three inches long.

Requirements — Prefers moist sites in full sun.

Habitat — Regions 1, 3, 4.

Bloom period — March through August.

Notes — Honey bees, bugs, butterflies and beetles feed on the nectar. The coneflower is a much desired ornamental. ❀

San Antonio Botanical Center Photo

Golden-eye Sunflower
Viguiera dentata

Description — An upright perennial that grows three-to-six feet tall and in clusters. The branches are slender and widely spreading. The stem has many branches.

Flower — The head of the flower is seven-eighths-to-one-inch-and-a-half across. There are 10-to-12 yellow ray flowers that are toothed at the tip. There are numerous disk flowers in a cluster. The heads are solitary, terminal and on a long, slender leafless stalk.

Leaves — Leaves are one-and-three-eighths-to-five inches long and three inches wide. They are opposite in the lower portion of the plant and alternate in the upper portion. They're stalked, the blade tapering at the base. The margins are sharp and coarsely toothed.

Requirements — Dry and calcareous soils.

Habitat — Regions 3, 5, 7, 10.

Bloom period — September through October

Notes — The plant has a somewhat musk-like odor. ❀

San Antonio Botanical Center Photo

Jack-in-the-pulpit
Arisaema triphyllum

Description — Perennial to 18 inches tall.

Flower — Odd-shaped flowers give rise to showy bright red berries three-eighths inches in diameter.

Leaves — Mostly two to three segments, sessile, elliptic up to nine inches long. Petioles up to two feet. Peduncle shorter than petiole, spathe 4–7 inches long, green to purple outside, tube long, inside variously striped purple and green or white, blade bent forward, spadix with sterile appendage nearly cylindrical, short, green to purple, slightly exerted beyond tube.

Requirements — They thrive in rich, well-drained soils high in organic matter. A hardy plant that can grow in shaded areas.

Habitat — Regions 1, 2.

Bloom period — May through June.

Notes — Great for woodland planting in shade and good soil. Also known as Indian turnip. ❁

San Antonio Botanical Center Photo

Jicamilla
Jatropha cathartica

Description — Perennial from a deep thickened woody root.

Flower — Reddish flowers are about one-quarter-of-an-inch wide and are born above blue-gray foliage.

Leaves — Leaves are alternate and deeply palmately lobed.

Requirements — Prefers clay soils in brush of prairies and plains.

Habitat — Regions 2, 6.

Bloom period — April through October.

Notes — It is often planted in pots perched above the soil to display the massive root. ❀

San Antonio Botanical Center Photo

Jimson Weed
Datura inoxia

Description — Plant grows to three feet tall.

Flower — Large funnel-shaped flowers to six inches long and almost as wide.

Leaves — Ovate to 10 inches long.

Requirements — Plenty of sun. They are annuals but can be perennial in mild winters.

Habitat — Regions 1, 2, 3, 4, 5, 6, 7, 8, 9, 10.

Bloom period — March through November.

Notes — Flowers, pollinated by hawkmoths, open in evening and close before noon the following day. Also known as Indian apple or angel's trumpet. ❀

Joe Pye Weed
Eupatorium fistulosum

Description — A tall perennial that grows three-to-nine feet tall.

Flower — Purple or lilac-pink flowers form at the stem tips.

Leaves — Leaves are mostly opposite, sometimes are whorled or alternate.

Requirements — Plenty of sun and water.

Habitat — Region 1.

Bloom period — July through August.

Notes — Plant attracts butterflies. ❁

San Antonio Botanical Center Photo

San Antonio Botanical Center Photo

Meadow-rue
Thalictrum species

Description — An upright perennial, the plant grows two-to-three feet tall. Purplish stems are thick near the base, branching in the upper portion of the plant.

Flower — Small greenish flowers grow in terminal clusters. The flower has four or five sepals that are petal-like, falling as they open. There are no petals. Its numerous colored stamens are thread-like, soon drooping and becoming entangled. Its few pistils are short and not showy.

Leaves — The leaves are alternate. The blade is divided into numerous leaflets. The leaflets are thick. The lower leaves are long-stalked while the upper leaves are stalkless.

Requirements — Prefers shade and fairly rich soil with a good supply of moisture.

Habitat — Regions 1, 2, 3, 4, 5, 7, 8, 9, 10.

Bloom period — March through May.

Notes — Plant grows in woodland areas. ❀

San Antonio Botanical Center Photo

Mealy Sage
Salvia farinacea

Description — This perennial grows to about two feet tall. The plant has the usual sage fragrance.

Flower — The blue flowers are five-lobed and two-lipped from two-thirds-of-an-inch to three-quarters-of-an-inch long. The flower has two stamens and one pistil.

Leaves — The long, narrow leaves grow in clusters out of which grow the flower stems. The leaves may or may not have teeth.

Requirements — Prefers full sun.

Habitat — Regions 2, 3, 4, 5, 6, 7, 8, 10.

Bloom period — April through November.

Notes — Plant is named for the mealy-white (sometimes purple) appearance of the sepals which are covered with felted hairs. ⚙

LBJ Wildflower Center Photo

Mexican Hat
Ratibida columnifera

Description — Rugged and aggressive sun-loving perennial grows to three feet tall.

Flower — The characteristic black, cone-shaped heads are surrounded by drooping fire-red ray flowers with a splash of yellow accent. There is one flower head to each stem.

Leaves — Leaves are alternate two to four-and-a-half inches long and are deeply cut into five to nine narrow segments. Both leaves and stems are somewhat rough, with the upper third of the stem bare.

Requirements — Prefers sun and well-drained soil. Outstanding in humid climates.

Habitat — Regions 1, 2, 3, 4, 5, 6, 7, 8, 9, 10.

Bloom period — April through October.

Notes — Available in several color variations. At maturity the upright branch stems may become somewhat woody. ❂

San Antonio Botanical Center Photo

Missouri Primrose
Oenothera missouriensis

Description — A hearty perennial, the native from Texas to Missouri, reaches a height of six to 14 inches. The closed flower is a shade of pink and drooping.

Flower — A prolific bloomer with a magnificent lemon-yellow flower blooms for several days. Blooms, up to four inches across, open in evening before sunset and stay open all night. Buds are green and speckled dark pink.

Leaves — Leaves are one-and-an-eighth-to-four inches long and up to an inch-and-a-quarter wide. The leaves are alternate, tapered at the base to a short stalk and rather thick in texture. The margins are entire, wavy or remotely toothed.

Requirements — Prefers well-drained soil in full sun.

Habitat — Dry, thin, rocky, exposed calcareous soils on prairies, cliffs, hillsides and slopes. Regions 4, 5, 7, 8, 9.

Bloom period — April through August.

Notes — The compact height makes this plant an excellent border plant and ground cover since it remains all year. Also known as fluttermill, it transplants well. ✿

San Antonio Botanical Center Photo

Missouri Violet
Viola missouriensis

Description — This low perennial grows up to six inches. It is stemless.

Flower — The showy flower has pale violet petals marked with purple around the white center.

Leaves — Leaves are egg-shaped to heart-shaped and are toothed.

Requirements — Prefers shade, plenty of moisture.

Habitat — Regions 1, 2, 3, 4, 5, 7, 8, 10.

Bloom period — March through May.

Notes — Plant suitable for rock and wild gardens as edging plants in the semi-shady border. ✺

San Antonio Botanical Center Photo

Mountain-mint
Pycnanthemum albescens

Description — A perennial to about four feet tall, the plant has small white or lavender flowers surrounded by large white bracts.

Flower — The bloom is two-lipped. The lower lip is three-lobed. There are four stamens in two pairs.

Leaves — Leaves are entire or toothed. There are two leaves at a node on opposite ends of the plant.

Habitat — Regions 1, 2, 3, 4.

Bloom period — June through October.

Notes — It has a pungent, mint-like odor when crushed, and stems are square in cross section. ❀

San Antonio Botanical Center Photo

Mullein
Verbascum thapsus

Description — A robust biennial now naturalized throughout the state, the plant grows on stalks up to six feet tall. The plant is upright, coarse, stout and a densely hairy perennial and grows in densely crowded clusters.

Flower — Yellow flowers are three-quarters-to-one-and-one-eighth inches across. Its five petals are united. The five stamens have red anthers.

Leaves — Four-to-15 inches long and mostly clustered at base, the leaves are alternate and stalkless. They basically extend down the stem as wings. Leaves are soft, prominently veined and densely covered with felt-like gray hair. Upper leaves are progressively smaller.

Requirements — Grows in most situations, especially pastures.

Habitat — Regions 1, 2, 3, 4, 5, 6, 7, 8, 9, 10.

Bloom period — March through November.

Notes — The plant is grown as much for its attractive foliage as the floral display. Seeds are sought after by songbirds. Several cultivars are available. Also known as cowboy toilet paper plant or flannel leaf. ❀

San Antonio Botanical Center Photo

Passion-vine
Passiflora lutea

Description — Slender vine that can grow to 10 feet or so.

Flower — Greenish-white or greenish-yellow flowers are about one-half-to-three-quarters-of-and-inch wide with five petals and five sepals.

Leaves — They grow to four inches, are three-lobed and wider than they are long.

Requirements — Prefers moist, shady, wooded areas.

Habitat — Regions 1, 2, 3, 4, 5, 6, 7.

Bloom period — May through September.

Notes — Many passiflora's have interesting relationships with certain butterfly species. Also known as yellow passion-flower. ❀

San Antonio Botanical Center Photo

Phlox
Phlox pilosa

Description — Stalwart old-fashioned perennial, the plant grows to about 12 inches tall. Covered with gland-tipped hairs, the slender, upright plant is sticky to touch. The stem is usually solitary, sometimes branching in the upper portion.

Flower — The slightly fragrant white, pink or lavender flower is three-quarters-of-an-inch long and about one-and-a-fourth inches across. The flower is tubular-shaped and is five-lobed at the rim. The lobes are wide-flaring, appearing almost flat. Flowers are found in clusters.

Leaves — Leaves grow to five inches long and one-quarter-of-an-inch wide. The leaves are broader in the upper portion of the stem. The leaves are opposite, stalkless and fringed with hairs.

Requirements — Grows in a variety of soils. Tolerates some shade.

Habitat — Regions 1, 2, 3, 4, 5, 7.

Bloom period — March through May.

Notes — The plant is pollinated by small bees and butterflies. ✿

San Antonio Botanical Center Photo

Pickerelweed
Pontederia cordata

   Description — An aquatic perennial to about three feet high, the creeping, root-like underground plant is rooted in mud beneath water with leaves and spikes of blue or white flowers extending above the water.

   Flower — To five-sixteenths across, it is funnel-shaped. The middle lobe of the upper lip has two yellow spots. Numerous flowers are crowded in a slender elongating spike to six inches.

   Leaves — Long-stalked with heart-shaped or lance-like blades.

   Requirements — Prefers full or partial shade.

   Habitat — In shallow calm water along edges of lazy waterways, sluggish bayous or in the fringe of freshwater marshes, swamps or lakes. Regions 1, 2, 3, 4, 7.

   Bloom period — June through September.

   Notes — Plants often form large colonies. ❂

San Antonio Botanical Center Photo

Pigeon Wings
Clitoria mariana

Description — A trailing, climbing perennial that can reach three feet tall, it is unbranched.

Flower — Its showy flowers are lilac and up to two inches across. The flower has 10 stamens, which are similar, united or have one that is separate.

Leaves — Leaves are rounded at both ends, broad in the middle to inversely ovate. Leaves are alternate and pinnate.

Requirements — Prefers sandy soils.

Habitat — Regions 1, 2, 3, 5, 7.

Bloom period — May through September.

Notes — There are about 30 species which are herbs or shrubs. They are native to warm regions. Also known as butterfly-pea. Also known as spoonflower. ❁

LBJ Wildflower Center Photo

Pink Evening Primrose
Oenothera speciosa

Description — Grows eight-to-18 inches high, the plant resembles tiny glowing lamps.

Flower — The bloom grows in a cluster at the end of the branches. The flowers are pink to rose-pink and occasionally white. They are cup-shaped, up to two inches across with four broad petals marked with dark pink veins. The center is greenish-yellow to rose pink. The four sepals are united into a slender tube below the petals, but are pushed open and back as the petals open.

Leaves — Leaves are alternate and are one-to-four inches long.

Requirements — Prefers rich, moist soils of fields and roadsides.

Habitat — Regions 1, 2, 3, 4, 5, 6, 7, 8, 10.

Bloom period — March through July.

Notes — Also known as showy primrose or buttercups. ❀

San Antonio Botanical Center Photo

Pitcher Plant
Sarracenia alata

Description — The plant is an insectivorous perennial bog plant that has an odd shape.

Flower — The flower hangs its head and looks directly to the ground. The bloom is attractive with five sepals and five petals, yellowish-green to light orange and one-and-a half inches across.

Leaves — Each large leaf forms a tube, larger at the top and sloping toward the base. The upper part of the leaf bends over the opening of the flower as if to protect it. The inner surface of the leaf is covered thickly with tiny hairs.

Requirements — Prefers damp, boggy areas.

Habitat — Regions 1, 3.

Bloom period — March through April.

Notes — The top part of the leaf has many small glands that exude a nectar that attracts insects. When they enter and then touch the slippery side of the tube, they drop to the bottom of the plant, where the plant secretes a liquid that dissolves the soft parts of their bodies and absorbs them. Also known as yellow trumpets. ✿

San Antonio Botanical Center Photo

Prairie Larkspur
Delphinium carolinianum

Description — Slender perennial that grows about one-to-three feet tall.

Flower — Color ranges from dark bluish to bluish-white.

Leaves — Alternate, broad leaves that are divided and lobed into many narrow segments.

Requirements — Prefers dry, open areas and full sun.

Habitat — Regions 1, 2, 3, 4, 5, 6, 7, 10.

Bloom period — April through July.

Notes — Also known as the blue larkspur. Larkspurs contain toxic alkaloids that should be considered deadly if ingested. Significant losses in cattle and sheep caused by the larkspur have sometimes been reported in western states. ❀

San Antonio Botanical Center Photo

Puccoon-gromwell
Lithospermum incisum

Description — This perennial from a stout-tap root with many above ground stems reaches 12 inches tall.

Flower — Tubular yellow flowers are an inch or more long. Flowers are often in clusters at the end of stems. They are trumpet-shaped with five petal-like lobes, which open to one inch across with crinkled margins.

Leaves — Leaves are alternate, two-to-four inches long with rolled edges. They are larger near the base.

Requirements — Prefers full sun and sandy soil.

Habitat — Regions 1, 2, 3, 4, 5, 6, 7, 8, 9, 10.

Bloom period — March through June.

Notes — The roots of the plant were used by Indians and settlers to produce red dye. A number of early medicinal applications have also been documented. ❁

Purple Coneflower
Echinacea purpurea

Description — Reliable and easy to grow, the rough and hairy perennial reaches two-to-three feet tall.

Flower — The head grows to six inches across. The ray flowers are rose-purple.

Leaves — Leaves are alternate and simple. Lower leaves are ovate to broadly lance-shaped, coarsely toothed and long-stalked. The upper leaves are narrower and nearly entire.

Requirements — Tolerates some shade and a wide variety of soils.

San Antonio Botanical Center Photo

Habitat — Region 1.

Bloom period — May through September.

Notes — Commercially grown for its medical properties. ❀

LBJ Wildflower Center Photo

Purple Horsemint
Monarda citriodora

Description — Tall annual, it is a typical member of the mint family that grows to three feet.

Flower — Has whorls of showy lavender flowers that stair-step up its distinctive square stems.

Leaves — Slender, often with serrated edges.

Requirements — Prefers full sunlight but can grow in various soil types. Can tolerate very dry conditions.

Habitat — Regions 1, 2, 3, 4, 5, 6, 7, 8, 9, 10.

Bloom period — April through October.

Notes — Flowers attract hummingbirds and swallowtail butterflies. The crushed leaves release a sweet citrus odor and can be used as a mosquito repellent when rubbed on the skin. Also known as lemon mint. ❀

San Antonio Botanical Center Photo

Purple Passionflower
Passiflora incarnata

Description — A trailing, climbing perennial vine, stems reach as high as 25 feet long and climb over bushes and fences.

Flower — The purple bloom, two-to-three inches across with fringed corona, is on short stalks from leaf axils. The five sepals and five petals look alike and are covered by the fringed corona of crimped filaments. The fruit is a two-to-three inch berry that turns orange-yellow when ripe. Five stamens unite in a tube at their bases and spread in the upper portion of the flower. The three-part pistil rises above the stamens.

Leaves — Leaves, three-to-five inches long, are alternate and are deeply three-lobed. They are dark green above and whitish below.

Requirements — Can grow in various soils such as pastures, fields, fence rows, along stream banks and edges of woodlands and thickets.

Habitat — Regions 1, 2, 3, 4, 5.

Bloom period — April through September.

Notes — Edible pulp can be sucked from the husk or made into juice or jelly, and tropical species are raised commercially for their fruits. Native Americans used the plant, also known as maypop, as a medicine. Research shows that extracts are mildly sedative, reduce blood pressure, increase respiratory rate and decrease activity. The fruits are potentially harmful if ingested in large amounts. ✸

San Antonio Botanical Center Photo

Purple Pleat-leaf
Alophia drummondii

Description — Upright, delicate, smooth perennial to one-foot tall, growing from a deep, globe-like bulb.

Flower — Bluish interesting flowers are about two inches across with six petal-like segments. Outer three segments are broad and wide-spreading, heavily spotted with violet and outlined with purple in basal portion. Inner three segments are much smaller and are blackish-violet in basal portion and violet near tip. Flowers are solitary or two or three at tip of leafless stem, emerging from a broad, sheathing, leaf-like bract.

Leaves — Up to 12 inches long, alternate, mostly basal, narrow and grass-like, folded together for most of length.

Requirements — Full sun or partial shade on sandy or clay soils in prairies, meadows, grasslands and open areas.

Habitat — Regions 1, 2, 3, 4, 5.

Bloom Period — March through May.

Notes — Also known as Herbertia. It is endemic to the southern portion of the state, but is usually abundant when found forming large areas of solid blue. ❀

LBJ Wildflower Center Photo

Rain-lily
Cooperia drummondii

Description — This upright perennial from an inedible bulb grows to about one-foot tall.

Flower — Flowers open in the evening and last three to four days before wilting. The six flaring, petal-like segments are white with a pinkish tinge on the outer surfaces. The tubular-shaped flower is about one-inch across and three-to-seven inches long.

Leaves — Leaves are slender and glass-like and can reach 12 inches long. Leaves are smooth and gray-green.

Requirements — Prefers generally clay or sandy soils in lawns, pastures, prairies, open woodlands and on hills and slopes.

Habitat — Regions 1, 2, 4, 6, 7.

Bloom period — May through September.

Notes — This plant usually blooms after it rains. It is pollinated by moths. ✿

San Antonio Botanical Center Photo

Rattlesnake Master
Eryngium yuccifolium

Description — The upright, coarse, hairy-stemmed biennial reaches two-to-four feet.

Flower — Round button-like terminal heads contain numerous small, greenish white flowers, each no more than one inch across, packed close together. They are surrounded by sharp-pointed leaf-like bracts.

Leaves — Leaves grow to 40 inches long, are alternate and finely divided into numerous opposite narrow segments appearing fern-like.

Most of the long leaves cluster at the base, while the smaller leaves clasp the stem.

Requirements — Thrives in sunny, moist terrain.

Habitat — Regions 1, 2, 3, 4.

Bloom period — May through August.

Notes — Also known as the button snakeroot. Poultices of the root were used for treatment of snakebite by Native Americans and settlers. The plant was also used to prevent whooping cough. ❀

Red-flowered Yucca
Hesperaloe parviflora

San Antonio Botanical Center Photo

Description — Succulent perennial that grows three-to-six feet tall and has a base of persistent thick dark green leaves.

Flower — From this basal rosette arises an open cluster of one-inch, pinkish-red thickish flowers scattered along the upper stem and bloom from the bottom up. The petals form a one-quarter-to-one-half inch long tube, fine-toothed at the opening and revealing a tip of yellow on the inside.

Leaves — There are many stiff, narrow, sharp-pointed leaves at the base, with margins that become frayed.

Requirements — Prefers dry, full sun.

Habitat — Regions 5, 7, 8, 10.

Bloom period — March through July.

Notes — Popular ornamental attractive to hummingbirds. It is used by the Texas State Highway Department in landscaping. ❁

San Antonio Botanical Center Photo

Red Prickly Poppy
Argemone sanguinea

Description — A short-lived perennial or biennial to about 48 inches tall, the plant has yellowish sap that easily rubs off. It is upright, smooth, but prickly.

Flower — To three-and-one-half inches across the bloom has four-to-six petals cupped.

Leaves — Two-to-six inches long, alternate, without stalks, leaves are blushing-green. The veins are conspicuously blue. Lower leaves are deeply lobed almost to midrib.

Requirements — Prefers full sun, sandy or silt-like soil.

Habitat — Various soils in disturbed areas, cultivated fields, range lands and chaparral plains. Found in colonies that often cover several acres. Regions 2, 6, 7, 10.

Bloom period — February through May.

Notes — These plants cannot be transplanted with any success, but can be raised from seed and should be used more in cultivation. If used as cut flowers, the stems should be seared over an open flame immediately after cutting. ✺

San Antonio Botanical Center Photo

Rock-nettle
Eucnide bartonioides

Description — Annual or weak perennial that grows about a foot tall.

Flower — Beautiful yellow flowers grow to more than an inch wide.

Leaves — Has many branches that usually spread on the ground with ovate, laciniate or lobed leaves.

Requirements — Full sun and good drainage.

Habitat — Regions 7, 10.

Bloom period — May through August.

Notes — Flowers open in late afternoon. About eight species of this flower are native to Southwest U.S. and Mexico. It deserves more widespread cultivation. ❁

San Antonio Botanical Center Photo

Rock Rose
Pavonia lasiopetala

Description — A shrubby perennial the plant grows to three-and-half feet tall.

Flower — The flower is one-and-a-half inches wide. Numerous blooms of ice-white, pink or rose-colored cover the plant.

Leaves — Leaves are alternate and prominently lobed at the base.

Requirements — Prefers full sun or partial shade and ample moisture.

Habitat — Regions 6, 7.

Bloom period — January through December.

Notes — This is a popular xeriscape plant. ✸

San Antonio Botanical Center Photo

Scrambled Eggs
Corydalis aurea

Description — Annual grows to about 10 inches tall. The plant has many stems.

Flower — The yellow flowers is about three-quarters-of-an-inch long. The spur is about half as long as the rest of the petal. The bracts are toothed.

Leaves — Leaves are three-pinnate, unbranched, elongated and terminal.

Requirements — Suitable in variety of soils.

Habitat — Regions 5, 7, 8, 9, 10.

Bloom period — February through September.

Notes — Plant is worthy of more extensive cultivation. ⚘

San Antonio Botanical Center Photo

Seaside Heliotrope
Heliotropium curassavicum

Description — A low, usually sprawling or trailing plant, the smooth short-lived herbaceous perennial is succulent, rubbery and reaches 16 inches long. Plants have a whitish coating that easily rubs off. Prostrate stems have bluish-green leaves.

Flower — Coiled-flower spikes to one-eighth of an inch across, the bloom is white or bluish with a yellow throat and has a funnel-shaped five-lobed rim.

Leaves — Three-eighths to two inches wide, the blade is thick, juicy and pale-green. It is short-stalked.

Requirements — Prefers full sun in well-drained soils.

Habitat — Sandy usually alkaline or saline soils of beaches, mud flats, gravel banks and dried lake beds or edges. Regions 2, 3, 5, 6, 7, 8, 9, 10.

Bloom period — March through November.

Notes — Densely flowered curls resemble monkey tails. Also known as monkey's tail heliotrope. ✺

Shooting Star
Dodecathleon meadia

Description — A perennial with white, pink or lilac colored flowers, the plant grows to 12 inches.

Flower — The five-merous flower has reflexed petals and stamens forming a pointed beak. Filaments are free or united. The yellow connectives are smooth.

Leaves — Leaves are ovate to spatula-shaped and up to 12 inches long.

Requirements — Prefers full sun or partial shade in well-drained soil.

Habitat — Regions 1, 3, 4, 5, 7.

San Antonio Botanical Center Photo

Bloom period — March through May.

Notes — Usually one of the first wildflowers to bloom in early spring. ❋

San Antonio Botanical Center Photo

Showy Buttercup
Ranunculus macranthus

Description — The plant is an early perennial to about one-foot tall, usually reclining to about three feet across. The stem is robust with coarse, rough hairs.

Flower — Flower has five sepals, reflexed to three-sixteenths-of-an-inch long. Eight to 18 petals are yellow, three-eighths to three-fourths-of-an-inch across.

Leaves — Leaflets are usually three-to-five inches long with larger leaves up to six inches long. Leaves are simple or compound.

Requirements — Favors wet spots and tolerates the shade.

Habitat — Regions 2, 3, 4, 5, 6, 7, 10.

Bloom period — March through June.

Notes — Petals often fall off the plant early. ✿

San Antonio Botanical Center Photo

Showy Palafoxia
Palafoxia hookeriana

Description — An annual that grows to six-feet tall.

Flower — Pink flowers are more than an inch wide.

Leaves — Grow to four inches and are rough on both sides.

Requirements — Prefers dry, sandy soils in prairies, pastures, hillsides and in woodlands openings.

Habitat — Regions 1, 3, 5.

Bloom period — September to October.

Notes — A showy flower that is worthy of more widespread cultivation. Though there is some dispute on the matter, most authorities believe the palafoxia takes its name from Jose de Palafox y Melzi, a Spanish general in the early 1800s who was noted for leading his armies against Napoleon. ❂

San Antonio Botanical Center Photo

Silver-leaf Nightshade
Solanum elaeagnifolium

Description — An upright perennial to almost three feet tall, the plant forms colonies from creeping roots.

Flower — Purple flowers reach one-inch long. There are five petals united at the base. The flower is five-lobed at the rim and appears star-shaped with large yellow antlers. Flowers are few in clusters from the leaf axils near the ends of branches.

Leaves — Leaves are six inches long, three-to-five times longer than wide. The leaves are alternate, long-stalked, gray-green in color and usually wavy-edged.

Requirements — Prefers dry soils in pastures, prairies and bottom lands.

Habitat — Regions 1, 2, 3, 4, 5, 6, 7, 8, 9, 10.

Bloom period — March through October.

Notes — Popular in Europe as an ornamental. Plant produces a berry that is yellow or a shade of black when ripe. It was used by Native Americans to make cheese. Also know as white horse-nettle. ❀

Skyrocket
Ipomopsis aggregata

Description — A biennial that grows to six feet tall.

Flower — Red tubular flowers can grow to be more than an inch long. Also can be golden-yellow, pink or nearly white.

Leaves — Leaves grow to two inches long and are pinnately dissected into linear segments.

Requirements — Prefers dry, sandy or rocky soils as well as shrubby brushlands or open wooded areas.

Habitat — Region 10.

Bloom period — June through October.

San Antonio Botanical Center Photo

Notes — Flowers frequently attract hummingbirds. Also known as the scarlet gilia. It is easily grown from seeds. ✸

San Antonio Botanical Center Photo

Snow-on-the-Mountain
Euphorbia marginata

Description — A stiffly upright, widely branching, hairy annual herb that ranges from 12 to 40 inches high. The plant features a solitary stem and is much-branching in the upper portion. The branches are paired or in threes.

Flower — Minute, 30–35 male and one female flower, are congested in a small, cup-like structure. The cup, with five white petal-like lobes, appears like a five-petal flower.

Leaves — Leaves range one-and-an-eighth to three-and-an-eighth inches long. Stem leaves are alternate and the upper leaves are opposite.

Requirements — Prefers well-drained soils. Usually found on clay, limestone or calcareous soils of range lands, gravel flats, arroyos and flood plains.

Habitat — Regions 1, 2, 3, 4, 5.

Bloom period — August through October.

Notes — When the stem is broken, the plant exudes a white milky sap that is irritating to the skin of some persons. ❀

San Antonio Botanical Center Photo

Solomon's Seal
Polygonatum biflorum

Description — Perennial with arching stems to three feet tall.

Flower — Greenish-white three-quarter-inch flowers hang in pairs under the stems.

Leaves — Alternate, opposite or whorled.

Requirements — Thrives in shady, deep, rich soil with plenty of water.

Habitat — Regions 1, 3, 4.

Bloom period — March through May.

Notes — Highly popular plant in wooded areas also known as King Solomon's Seal. ❀

San Antonio Botanical Center Photo

Spider Lily
Hymenocallis liriosme

Description — Much branched, upright and smooth perennial that grows to two feet tall.

Flower — Flowers are about eight inches across. They grow in clusters of three-to-seven at the top of a leafless stalk.

Leaves — Shiny, strap-like leaves, up to 30 inches long, appear with the flower stalk that grows from a large bulb. Leaves are pale green.

Requirements — Prefers freshwater marshes and wet ditches.

Habitat — Regions 1, 2, 3, 4.

Bloom period — March through May.

Notes — The blooms usually open successively, so the plant remains in bloom for many days. ✿

LBJ Wildflower Center Photo

Spiderwort
Tradescantia species

Description — Plants are usually erect. They often grow in clumps.

Flower — The flowers grow in umbel-like clusters with one-to-three-leaf-like bracts. There are three sepals and three light-blue to rose-violet or occasionally pure pink or white petals and six stamens.

Leaves — The leaves are alternate, often long and narrow.

Requirements — Prefers sunny points in open woods and prairies.

Habitat — Regions 1, 2, 3, 4, 5, 6, 7, 8, 9, 10.

Bloom period — March through June.

Notes — Found in most soils, often at the edges of woods. Difficult to distinguish between the species because they often hybridize. ❀

San Antonio Botanical Center Photo

Spotted Beebalm
Monarda punctata

Description — Tall annual, biennial or weak perennial that grows to three feet.

Flower — Has whorls of whitish or yellowish flowers around the stem.

Leaves — Grow one-to-four inches and are lance-like and shallowly toothed.

Requirements — Prefer dry, sandy soils.

Habitat — Regions 1, 2, 3, 4, 5, 6, 7, 8, 9, 10.

Bloom period — March through July.

Notes — It is a highly variable species with nine varieties listed in Texas. Native American tribes were known to use tea from spotted beebalm leaves for colds, fevers, stomach cramps and coughs. Also known as horse mint. ✿

San Antonio Botanical Center Photo

Straggler Daisy
Calyptocarpus vialis

Description — A hardy sprawling stem to two feet long. Each plant contains a few yellow ray flowers and three or four yellow disk flowers. The solitary head is located on a weak, branching stem.

Flower — The head is only one-quarter-of-an inch across with a few yellow rays and disk flowers.

Leaves — Ovate leaves reach one-to-two inches long and have serrate margins. They occur in pairs along the stem and are opposite.

Requirements — Plant grows in most soils.

Habitat — Regions 2, 3, 4, 5, 6, 7.

Bloom period — February through December.

Notes — Also known as lawnflower and horse-weed, it is native to Mexico, Central America and the West Indies. ✿

San Antonio Botanical Center Photo

Summer Poinsettia
Euphorbia cyathophora

Description — Annual to about three-feet tall.

Flower — Cyathia comes in terminal clusters with one or two broad glands, more or less two-lipped with opening narrowly oblong.

Leaves — Variable, ovate to linear or sometimes fiddle-shaped, entire or toothed, glossy green, upper leaves and bracts are red or red-based.

Requirements — Needs full sun growing conditions or plants become leggy.

Habitat — Regions 2, 3, 4, 5, 6, 7, 8, 10.

Bloom period — Showy bracts are formed May through September.

Notes — Also known as fire-on-the-mountain, painted leaf or Mexican fire plant. Sometimes grown in flower gardens and often naturalized. ❁

San Antonio Botanical Center Photo

Swan Flower
Aristrolochia longiflora

Description — A perennial, it is a low growing or trailing plant forming a clump one foot or more across.

Flower — Odd-shaped flowers are up to five inches long.

Leaves — Grass-like leaves rise from a thick fragrant tap root.

Requirements — Plenty of sun.

Habitat — Regions 2, 3, 6, 7, 8.

Bloom period — March through November.

Notes — Foliage is often eaten away by pipevine shallow-tail butterfly larvae. ❁

San Antonio Botanical Center Photo

Sweet Sand Verbena
Abronia fragrans

Description — Upright or widely sprawling, this sticky-haired low perennial grows to about 40 inches long. There are numerous stems and the plant is much-branched. It is often whitish in color.

Flower — Clusters of pink to lavender blooms are shaped like a long funnel. The flower, three-eighths-to-one-and-an-eighth inches, is deeply lobed around the rim. There are numerous flowers in a round-like cluster at the end of a branch.

Leaves — The leaves are two-to-four inches long and are opposite. Leaves are stalked and in pairs of unequal size. The blade is thin and rounded at both ends.

Requirements — Prefers sandy soils.

Habitat — Regions 5, 7, 8, 9, 10.

Bloom period — March through August.

Notes — Flowers open in the late afternoon and close the next morning. ❁

Texas Milkweed
Asclepias texana

Description — A beautiful perennial that grows to two feet tall.

Flower — Pure white flowers form in clusters.

Leaves — Long, narrow and opposite, they grow to five inches long.

Requirements — Grows in dry open woods, canyons or near streams.

Habitat — Regions 7, 10.

Bloom period — May through September.

Notes — Attracts butterflies and should be considered for far wider cultivation. ✿

San Antonio Botanical Center Photo

San Antonio Botanical Center Photo

Texas Plume
Ipomopis rubra

Description — A strictly upright biennial that grows to six feet.

Flower — A bright red tubular flower that rises from a single stalk reaches one to one-and-a-quarter inches long. The five petals are united at the base. Numerous flowers form a long, thick spike, opening from the tip of the stem downward.

Leaves — Leaves are in a small basal rosette also crowded on the stem. The leaves are alternate and the blade is deeply divided into 11–17 thread-like segments and appearing feathery or fern-like.

Requirements — Prefers full sun and drying sites.

Habitat — Regions 1, 2, 3, 4, 5, 7, 8.

Bloom period — June through October.

Notes — Plants, prized as cut-flowers, attract hummingbirds. Also known as standing cypress. ❁

San Antonio Botanical Center Photo

Texas Sage
Salvia texana

Description — A perennial that is covered with stiff hairs.

Flower — The sage has attractive purplish-blue flowers that form about one inch long.

Leaves — Opposite, stalked and sharply toothed, the leaves grow to two-and-a-half inches.

Requirements — Usually growing in dry or stony sites.

Habitat — Regions 2, 4, 5, 6, 7, 8, 9, 10.

Bloom period — March through October.

Notes — Frequently found on limestone rocks in western and central Texas. ❁

LBJ Wildflower Center Photo

Texas Star
Lindheimera texana

Description — Plants grow six-to-24 inches tall and are widely branched. Stems and branches are hairy.

Flower — Each flower head has five bright yellow ray flowers, each with two prominent veins and indented with the tip. Flower heads are one-to-one-and-a-quarter inch across.

Leaves — Lower leaves are alternate and coarsely toothed, but the upper ones are opposite and smooth on the edges two-to-two-and-a-half inches long.

Requirements — Prefers woods and prairies.

Habitat — Regions 2, 3, 4, 5, 7, 8.

Bloom period — March through May.

Notes — Found in open areas. There can be several flower heads in each cluster at the end of each stem. ❂

Texas Tuberose
Manfreda maculosa

Description — Perennial up to three-feet tall with a basal rosette of succulent green leaves spotted with purple.

Flower — Two-inch tubular flowers open white and fade to magenta

Leaves — Grow to one foot long and three-quarters inch wide.

Requirements — Full sun or filtered shade.

Habitat — Regions 2, 3, 4.

Bloom period — April through July

Notes — Deserves more attention as an ornamental. ❁

San Antonio Botanical Center Photo

Texas Vervain
Verbena halei

LBJ Wildflower Center Photo

Description — This tall and erect perennial is also known as the slender vervain. It reaches one-to-two-and-a-half feet tall with several branches in the upper part.

Flower — Flowers grow in long, loose clusters, blooming around the stem from the bottom up. There are usually six-to-20 flowers blooming at a time. The blue-to-lavender bloom is a quarter-of-an-inch across. The flower is trumpet-shaped, ending in five petal-like lobes.

Leaves — The leaves vary. The upper leaves are slightly toothed or sometimes with smooth margins. The lower leaves are deeply cut in some cases. Leaves are three-fourths-of-an-inch-to-three inches long and one-and-a-half inches wide.

Requirements — Prefers full sun.

Habitat — Regions 1, 2, 3, 4, 5, 6, 7, 8, 9, 10.

Bloom period — March through June.

Notes — This plant is hard to identify. To make it clear that the plant is a member of the Verbena species, check the way the tiny flowers grow on the stem. ❁

San Antonio Botanical Center Photo

Tube-tongue
Siphonoglossa pillosella

Description — This low, upright or sprawling hairy perennial grows usually less that one foot from a woody base.

Flower — Up to one inch long, it features a white to rose or pale violate to dark lavender bloom with two lips. The lower lip is large, up to one-half inch across, three-lobed, purple-dotted and with a white spot in the throat of the tube. Flowers are solitary or few, born in axils of the upper leaves.

Leaves —Three-eighths-of-an-inch to an-inch-and-five-eighths long to three-fourths of an inch wide, the leaves are opposite, stalkless or almost so, and entire.

Requirements — Prefers dry rocky or gravel-like soil. It is often shaded, in pastures and woodlands.

Habitat — Regions 2, 6, 7, 10.

Bloom period — April through October.

Notes — This plant can be used as a border plant and also acts as a good soil binder. Also known as false-honeysuckle because of its similarity to true honeysuckle. ❂

San Antonio Botanical Contor Photo

Venus Looking-glass
Triodanis species

Description — Annual with purplish flowers on a terminal spike, the plant is upright or somewhat sprawling, thin, succulent, slender stemmed one-to-two feet tall.

Flower — One inch or more across with the bloom closing early in day, there are three petals, two of equal size and the third quite inconspicuous or absent. The buds are clustered in a boat-shaped terminal spate. The blooms open one at a time.

Leaves — To six inches long and one-inch wide, the leaves are toothed, clasping or sessile, alternate and mostly in basal cluster. They are flat or grooved along midrib, hairy on upper surface and somewhat rough to the touch.

Requirements — Prefers shade.

Habitat — Sandy or clay soils in almost all habitats including limestone slopes, open pinelands, abandoned pastures, stream banks, thicket or woodlands. Regions 1, 2, 3, 4, 5, 6, 7, 8, 10.

Bloom period — April through July.

Notes — Stems are angled, usually unbranched and covered with short hairs. ❁

Western Ironweed
Vernonia baldwinii

Description — This upright, tough and hairy perennial grows from three to five feet tall. Stems, often several, form clumps. Sometimes there are few to no branches in the flowering portion.

Flower — The plant blooms in clusters of small, purplish flowers. There are 18-to-34 disk flowers per head. Each head is surrounded by several purplish-green-like bracts, bending outward from sharp-pointed tips. The heads form a large compact terminal cluster.

Leaves — Three-and-a-fourth-to-six inches long and three-fourths-to-two-and-one-fourth inches wide, the leaves are alternate, stalkless and have sharply toothed margins.

San Antonio Botanical Center Photo

Requirements — Prefers moist or wet sites and rich sandy or clay soils.

Habitat — Regions 1, 2, 3, 4, 5, 7, 8, 9.

Bloom period — May through August.

Notes — The plant spreads by underground runners forming small colonies. ❁

San Antonio Botanical Center Photo

White-top Sedge
Rhynchospora colorata

Description — Perennial sedge ranging from 12-to-32 inches tall.

Flower — Globe-like heads of tiny flowers stemming from green and white bracts. It has three-to-six leafy bracts, with the white bases occupying one-tenth to one-third of their length. Flowers are minute.

Leaves — Leaves are grass-like.

Requirements — Full sun or partial shade on moist sites.

Habitat — Regions 1, 2, 3, 4, 6, 7, 8.

Bloom period — March through August.

Notes — This is from the sedge family, which are abundant in wetland habitats. ❁

Wild Buckwheat
Eriogonum annuum

Description — An annual or biennial that grows to five feet tall, the plant usually forms extensive stands as is quite showy.

Flower — About a quarter-inch across, white or pink. There are no petals, but the flower has six petal-like sepals in two rows.

Leaves — Leaves are one-to-three inches long and are alternate. They are short-stalked and narrow at the base. The margins are entire.

Requirements — Prefers full sun and dry, sandy or gravel-type soils in abandoned areas, old fields, pastures and plains.

San Antonio Botanical Center Photo

Habitat — Regions 1, 2, 3, 4, 5, 6, 7, 8, 9, 10.

Bloom period — April through November.

Notes — Flowers are numerous forming a flat-topped cluster. ✺

San Antonio Botanical Center Photo

Wild Honeysuckle
Gaura lindheimeri

Description — Upright to widely spreading, this soft-hairy slender perennial reaches two feet tall. Stems are much-branched in the upper portion of the plant, solitary to several from the base.

Flower — The flower is about an inch across and is long and white, turning pink with age. There are four petals in one row on the upward side and eight conspicuously long, red-tipped stamens, upright to drooping opposite on the petals.

Leaves — Leaves are one-quarter-to-three-and-a-fourth inches long to one-half inch wide. Leaves are alternate, stalkless, entire or with scattered teeth. Upper leaves are much smaller.

Requirements — Prefers rich clay or sandy soils.

Habitat — Regions 1, 2, 3, 4.

Bloom period — April through November.

Notes — Available in pink-flowered form, the wild honeysuckle is also known as white gaura. ❀

LBJ Wildflower Center Photo

Wild Onion
Allium drummondii

Description — A bulb plant, the wild onion can reach 12 inches tall. It is densely clustered.

Flower — The small flowers vary in color from white, pink to red.

Leaves — Leaves are usually narrow, up to one-eighth-of-an-inch wide. They are one-nerved and ovate-to-lance-shaped.

Requirements — Prefers open and grassy areas.

Habitat — Regions 1, 2, 3, 4, 5, 6, 7, 8, 9, 10.

Bloom period — March through May.

Notes — It often forms bulbils replacing the pedicels. ❀

LBJ Wildflower Center Photo

Windflower
Anemone heterophylla

Description — Tuberous rooted perennial grows to about 12 inches.

Flower — Flowers are an inch across and range in color from white to blue-lavender or violet with 10 sepals. They bloom in the morning or during very cloudy weather.

Leaves — Leaves are deeply divided and lobed.

Requirements — Full sun or shade.

Habitat — Regions 2, 3, 4, 5, 6, 7, 8, 10.

Bloom period — February through April.

Notes — Also known as granny's nightcap or basket anemone. They are of the buttercup family. ❁

Winecup
Callirhoe species

Description — A perennial either prostrate or upright that grows to about three feet depending on moisture and soil. The plant has gray-green stems.

Flower — Flowers have five petals that are cup-shaped at first and opening out nearly flat as the flower matures. They are one-to-two inches across. The stamens and pistil form a cone-like structure in the center of the flower.

Leaves — The basal leaves are alternate and have stems about as long as the leaves. The leaves are coarsely lobed or scalloped to deeply five-lobed. There are a few leaves on the upper part of the stem.

LBJ Wildflower Center Photo

Requirements — Prefers open or grassy areas on a wide variety of soils.

Habitat — Regions 1, 2, 3, 4, 5, 6, 7, 8, 9.

Bloom period — February through June.

Notes — There are several species of Callirhoe in Texas varying in color: cherry-red, pink and white. ❀

San Antonio Botanical Center Photo

Woolly Rose-mallow
Hibiscus lasiocarpus

Description — This perennial grows three to five feet tall and has hairy stems and leaves.

Flower — Large white and sometimes pinkish blossoms are three-to-four inches long, with a crimson eye at the center. Petals fold up at night and appear as though they had never been open.

Leaves — Toothed and alternate with long stems from four-to-six inches. Stems are woody and brittle.

Requirements — Swampy and damp areas.

Habitat — Regions 1, 2, 3, 7, 8.

Bloom period — July through October.

Notes — Also known as false cotton because it's flower resumes that of a cotton plant, which is in the same family. ❀

San Antonio Botanical Center Photo

Yellow Columbine
Aquilegia hinckleyana

Description — A perennial with long limbs of petals usually rounded at the apex.

Flower — Bright yellow two-inch plus flowers with spreading sepals.

Leaves — Rosette of blue-green or basal leaves.

Requirements — Prefers partial sun or dry shade. All columbines do well in rock gardens and perennial borders.

Habitat — Region 10.

Bloom period — March through May and often sporadically into November.

Notes — Widely cultivated under the name Texas gold, columbines cross readily with other related species. Plant may sporadically bloom into November. ❀

WILDFLOWER
CALENDAR OF EVENTS

March – April

La Grange Bluebonnet and Wildflower Trials — La Grange.

Country trails featuring bluebonnets, buttercups, Indian paint brush, daisies, dandelions, Mexican hats, violets and lemon mint.

For more information, write:
La Grange Area Chamber of Commerce, 171 S. Main, La Grange, 78945, or call 800-524-7264.

• • •

March 7–8 and 14–15

Gay-feather

San Antonio Botanical Center Photo

River Oaks Garden Club Azalea Trail — Houston.

Trail takes visitors through elegant homes and gardens in River Oaks and Tangelwood and the Bayou Bend Collection and Gardens.

For more information, call: River Oaks Garden Club at 713-523-2483.

• • •

Mid-March through early April

Wild Azalea Canyons — Newton County.

Wild azaleas or wild honeysuckle reaches its peak blooming period mid-to-late March.

For more information, write:
Newton County Chamber of Commerce, P.O. Box 66, Newton, 75966, or call 409-379-5527.

• • •

March 20 – April 5

Azalea and Spring Flower Trail — Tyler.
Seven miles of residential gardens and historic home sites, Arts and crafts.
For more information, write: Tyler Convention and Visitors Bureau,
407 N. Broadway, Tyler, 75702, or call 800-235-5712.

• • •

March 27

Spring Wildflower Identification — Houston.
Deadline to register for spring wildflower identification course taught by Dr. Larry Brown.
For more information, call:
Vines Environmental Science Center 713-365-4175.

San Antonio Botanical Center Photo

Purple passionflower

• • •

March 28

Brenham Downtown Spring Festival — Brenham.
Celebrate arrival of bluebonnets and spring. Arts and crafts from more than 100 exhibitors.
For more information, call: Brenham Downtown Association 409-836-3424.

• • •

March 29

Jasper Azalea Festival — Jasper.
Festival includes azalea trail, arts and crafts and other events.
For more information, call: Jasper Chamber of Commerce 409-384-2762.

• • •

April

Yoakum Wildflower Trail — Yoakum.
Open throughout the month for self-guided tours. Guided tours are available for clubs and groups April 1–14.

For more information, call: Allene Boening, 512-293-5224.
For a map of the trails, write:
Yoakum Chamber of Commerce, P.O. Box 591, Yoakum, 77995,
or call 512-293-2309.

• • •

April

DeWitt County Lanes and Byways — Cuero.
Celebration throughout month with wildflower exhibits and a wildflower drive.
For more information, write:
DeWitt County Wildflower Association, P.O. Box 995, Cuero, 77954,
or call 512-275-9942.

• • •

April – May

La Grange/Fayette County Wildflower Trails — La Grange.
Colorful spring wildflower trails.
For more information, write:
La Grange Area Chamber of Commerce, 129 N. Main, La Grange, 78945,
or call 409-968-5756.

• • •

April 4–5

Highland Lakes Bluebonnet Trails Festival — Buchanan Dam.
An arts and crafts festival scheduled in conjunction with the bluebonnet
trails viewing.
For more information, visit or write:
Buchanan Dam Chamber of Commerce, P.O. Box 282,
Buchanan Dam, 78609, or call 512-792-2803.

• • •

April 4–5

Official State of Texas Bluebonnet Festival — Washington County.
Event is highlighted by more than 125 arts and crafts exhibitors.
For more information, call:
The Chappell Hill Historical Society 409-836-6033, 409-277-1122,
or 1-800-225-3695.

• • •

April 18

Wildflower Day at LBJ State Park — LBJ State Park.
Lecture on planting, organized walks and plant identification displays.
Hours: 10 a.m. to 3 p.m. Park is open year round.
For more information, call: 830-644-2252.

• • •

April 18–19

Wildflower Days Festival — Lady Bird Johnson Wildflower Center, Austin.
Festival features lectures, wildflower walks, advice on native plant landscaping,
live music, activities for children and a native plant sale.
For more information, contact:
Lady Bird Johnson Wildflower Center, 512-292-4200.

• • •

April 19

Native Plants for a Houston Landscape — Houston Arboretum & Nature
Center.
An Urban Nature Series presented by Glenn Olden of the Native Plant Society,
Houston Chapter, 1 p.m. to 3 p.m.
For more information, write:
Houston Arboretum & Nature Center, 4501 Woodway, Houston, 77024,
or call 713-681-8433.

• • •

April 19

Guided Nature Tours — Houston Arboretum & Nature Center.
Free tours start at 2 p.m. and 3 p.m.
For more information, write:
Houston Arboretum & Nature Center, 4501 Woodway, Houston, 77024,
or call 713-681-8433.

• • •

April 23–25

Wildflower Trails of Texas — Hughes Springs.
Region is home to more than 1000 types of wildflower. A festival including
fun run, bicycle race, carnival and other events also is held.
For more information, write:
George Fite, Wildflower Trails of Texas, P.O. Box 805,
Hughes Springs, 75656, or call 903-639-7519, or fax to 903-639-3769.

April 25

Earth Day — Houston Arboretum & Nature Center.
Native plants for sale with proceeds to benefit the center's educational programs. Master Gardeners from Harris County Extension Service will be available to answer questions. No admission fee charged.
For more information, write:
　　Houston Arboretum & Nature Center, 4501 Woodway, Houston, 77024, or call 713-681-8433.

· · ·

April 26

Guided Nature Tours — Houston Arboretum & Nature Center.
Free tours start at 2 and 3 p.m.
For more information, write:
　　Houston Arboretum & Nature Center, 4501 Woodway, Houston, 77024, or call 713-681-8433.

· · ·

October 15–18

Tyler Rose Festival — Tyler.
Annual event since 1933, this tradition includes rose show and other festivities.
For more information, write:
　　Tyler Rose Festival Association, P.O. Box 8224, Tyler, 75711;
　　Tyler Rose Museum, 420 South Rose Park, Tyler, 75711,
　　or call 903-597-3130; or Tyler Convention and Visitors Bureau,
　　407 N. Broadway, Tyler, 75702, or call 800-235-5712.

· · ·

All Year

Big Bend National Park — West Texas.
Wildflowers are blooming somewhere in Big Bend all year.
For more information, call:
　　Big Bend National Park at 915-477-2251.

NATIVE PLANT RESOURCES

Anderson Landscape and Nursery
2222 Pech
Houston 77055
713-984-1342

The Antique Rose Emporium
9300 Lueckemeyer Rd.
Brenham 77833
409-836-5548

Barton Springs Nursery
3601 Bee Cave Rd.
Austin 78746
512-328-6655

Brazos Rim Farm, Inc.
433 Ridgewood
Fort Worth 76107
817-740-1184; Fax 817-625-1327
Contact: Pat Needham

Buchanan's Native Plants
611 E. 11th Street
Houston 77008
713-861-5702

Chaparral Estates Gardens
Rt. 1, Box 425
Killeen 76542
254-526-3973
Contact: Ken and Rita Schoen

Country Petals
Rt. 1, Box 137A, Houston St.
New Ulm 78950
409-992-3532; 713-461-3489
Contact: Betsy Arriola
Visit gardens, appt. only

Desert Floralscapes
105 Lindbergh
El Paso 79932
915-584-0433
Contact: Teresa Cavareta

Discount Trees of Brenham
2800 North Park Dr.
Brenham 77833
409-836-7225

Ecotone Gardens
806 Pine-Hwy. 69
Kountze 77625
409-246-3070

Gunsight Mountain Ranch and Nursery
Williams Creek Rd., Box 86
Tarpley 78883
830-562-3225; Fax 562-3266

Houston Garden Centers
FM 1960-Jones Rd. Area
10815 FM 1960 West
Houston 77064
281-897-0882

Northwest
2732 W. 18th
Houston 77008
713-869-8870

North Loop
2811 Airline Dr.
Houston 77009
713-869-9505

Town & Country
919 W. Sam Houston Pkwy. N
Houston 77079
713-973-1478

Katy
1436 Fry Rd.
Houston 77084
281-578-9590

Humble
5502 FM 1960 East
Humble 77346
281-812-4840

Westchase Area
11933 A. Westheimer
Houston 77056
281-759-2984

Woodlands
24800 I-45 North
Houston 77386
281-298-2082

Mission Bend Area
7209 Hwy 6 South
Houston 77084
281-568-9841

West University
5000 Southwest Frwy
Houston 77056
713-626-1849

Stafford Meadows
11829 Southwest Frwy
Houston 77031
281-495-6662

Cypress Station
435 FM 1960
Houston 77090
281-893-1172

Copperfield-Bearcreek
6072 Hwy 6 North
Houston 77084
281-463-8815

Lake Olympia
7225 Hwy 6 South
Sugar Land 77479
281-499-8488

Kings Creek Gardens
813 Stratus Rd.
Cedar Hill 75104
Fax 972-293-0920

Landscape Marketplace
1031 Austin Hwy
San Antonio 78209
210-822-1335

Lowrey Nursery
P.O. Box 1036
Montgomery 77356
409-449-4040

Love Creek Nursery
P.O. Box 1401
Medina 78055
830-589-2588
Contact: Carol & Baxter Adams

Madrone Nursery
2318 Hilliard
San Marcos 78666
512-353-3944

Redentas Organic Garden Center
2001 Skillman St.
Dallas 75206
214-823-9421

Native American Seed
127 N. 16th
Junction 76849
915-446-3600 or 915-446-4537

Native Resources Inc.
Rt. 1, Box 7J, on FM 971
Georgetown 78626
512-930-3935; Fax 512-930-5194

Natives of Texas
Spring Canyon Ranch
6520 Medina Hwy
Kerrville 78028
830-896-2169 or 830-698-3736
Contact: Betty Winningham

Native Texas Nursery
1004 MoPac Circle #101
Austin 78746
512-280-2824

North Haven Gardens
7700 Northaven Rd.
Dallas 75230-3297
214-363-5316

Organic + Nursery
10568 N. River Crossing
Waco 76712
254-776-6069
Contact: Reid Lewis

Park Place Gardens
2710 Hancock Dr.
Austin 78731
512-458-5909
10% discount to NPSOT members

Pots and Plants
5902 Bee Cave Rd.
Austin 78727
512-327-4564

The Rustic Wheelbarrel
416 W. Ave. D.
San Angelo 76903
915-659-2130

Schumacher's Hill Ctry. Gardens Inc.
588 FM Hwy 1863
New Braunfels 78132
210-620-5149

Southwest Landscape and Nursery
2220 Sandy Lake Rd.
Carrollton 75006
972-245-4557

Teas Tree Factory
32920 Decker Prairie Rd.
Magnolia 77355
281-356-2336

Texas Blooms Organic Garden
5016 Miller Ave.
Dallas 75206
214-328-1499
Contact: Patty Lancaster

Texzen Gardens
4806 Burnet Rd.
Austin 78756
512-454-6471

Thompson-Hills Nursery
Hwy 64 W. of Loop 323
Tyler 76504
903-597-9951

Vaughn's Nursery and Garden
15647 Ave. C
Channelview 77530
281-452-7369

Weston Gardens in Bloom Inc.
8101 Anglin Dr.,
Fort. Worth 76140
817-572-0549

Wetland Habitat Nursery
1430 Settegast Ranch Rd.
Richmond 77469
281-496-5544
Contact: Ennis or Harrie Cooley

Wichita Valley Landscape
5314 SW Parkway
Wichita Falls 76310
940-696-3082
Contract: Paul or Nila
10% discount to NPSOT members

Wildseed Farms, Inc.
1101 Campo Rosa Rd.
Eagle Lake 77434
800-848-0078; Fax 409-234-7407

Wolfe Nurseries
13802 Murphy Rd.
Stafford 77477
281-261-0252

3600 S.E. Beltway 8
Pasadena 77505
281-487-9783

916 S. Mason Rd.
Katy 77450
281-392-7399

1445 W. Bay Area Blvd.
Webster 77598
281-338-2050; Fax 281-338-2050

25598 Interstate 45
Spring 77386
281-367-2013

22205 Eastex Frwy
Humble 77339
281-358-6688

103939 Katy Frwy
Houston 77079
713-467-0301

4545 Beechnut
Houston 77096
713-665-6852

1616 W. Loop North
Houston 77008
713-868-1165

Glossary of Botanical Terms

Alkaline — Having a high exchangeable content of sodium, enough to interfer with the growth of most plants.

Alternate — Placed singly at different heights on the stem not opposite or whorled, between other organs or plant parts.

Annual — A plant that completes its entire life cycle within one year.

Anther — The tip of the stamen that holds a flower's pollen.

Areole — A spot in the form of a pit or a raised area on the surface of a cactus through which spines or other structures grow.

Axil — The juncture of a leaf or flower with a stalk or main stem.

Basal — Leaves located at the base of the main stem.

Biennial — Any plant that takes two years to mature.

Blade — Expanded portion of a leaf or petal.

Bract — A modified leaf subtending a flower, sometimes appearing as a scale-like or thread-like structure.

Calcareous — Soil high in calcium carbonate and limestone.

Clasping — Basal portion of a leaf or other organ partly or wholly surrounding the stem or other structure, but not united.

Corm — A short, fleshy underground stem, broader than high, producing stem from the base and leaves and flower stems from the top.

Cut — Sharply incised.

Cuttings — A term for one of several means of propagation.

Disk Flower — The small tubular flower found on the central disk of a composite-type flower head.

Dormant — Resting period of plant growth that occurs between fall of leaves and swelling of buds.

Endemic — Restricted to a limited geographic area.

Entire — Margins without teeth, lobes or incisions.

Farinaceous — Containing or rich in starch.

Funnel Shape — Tubular at the base, gradually flaring upward.

Herbaceous — A non-woody plant that dies to the ground in winter and resume growth in spring.

Hybrid — A plant grown from seed obtained by applying pollen from one variety or species on the stigma of another. Many valuable plants are produced by crossing species.

Inflorescence — Complete flower cluster or flower head, including bracts.

Lanceolate — Long and narrow, tapering toward the tip.

Leaflet — A leaf separated completely into two or more parts, appearing as a small leaf.

Lobe — A deeply indented part of a leaf or flower that does not break the continuity of the structure.

Margin — Outer edge of a somewhat flattened structure, as in the edge of a leaf.

Node — A joint on a stem where branches, leaves or flower stalks are attached.

Opposite — Two like parts connected at the same place but across from each other, such as leaves on opposite sides of the same stem.

Palmate — Divided or radiating from one point, three or more fingers spread, resembling a hand with the finger spread.

Pinnate — Leaflets on each side of a petiole forming a compound leaf.

Pistil — Female flower reproductive parts (ovary, style and stigma)

Pollen — Male spores borne by the anther.

Raceme — Spike-like inflorescence bearing evenly short-stalked flowers.

Ray Flowers — Outer petal-like flowers often surrounding the disk of the sunflower family.

Rosette — Circular cluster of leaves radiating from the stem at or near the ground.

Sepals — A leaf-like segment of the calyx.

Sessile — Attached without a stalk.

Spathe — A bract that encloses a flower or cluster.

Spike — Stalkless flowers opening up a long, central unbranched stem. Flowers are attached directly to main stem. Youngest flowers or buds are at the top.

Stamens — Male pollen-bearing reproductive structure, including filaments and anthers.

Stem — The main stalk of a plant arising from the roots.

Taproot — Primary root from which small later roots grow.

Teeth — Small notches of the leaf margin.

Tepals — Collective terms for sepals and petals when sepals are petal-like, as in Cooperia pedunculata (rain lily).

Tube, Tubular — Hollow, near-uniform in width, longer than wide, circular in cross-section.

Two-lipped — A flower that has an upper and lower division.

Umbel — An often flat-topped inflorescence with stems rising from a common point.

Whorl — Three or more leaves, bracts or flowers arranged in a circle around a stem.

Index

Abbott, Carroll, 10, 12, 13, 40, 41
abronia fragrans, 127
Alholm, Patricia, 21, 23, 24
allium drummondii, 140
alophia drummondii, 105
anemone heterophylla, 141
angel's trumpet, 83
antelope-horns, 45
aquilegia canadensis, 67
aquilegia hinckleyana, 144
argemone sanguinea, 109
arisaema triphyllum, 81
aristolochia, 31
artemisia ludoviciana, 69
asclepias, 31
asclepias asperula, 45
asclepias curassavica, 51
asclepias texana, 128
asclepias tuberosa, 55
ashe juniper, 23
atristrolochia longiflora, 126
basket anemone, 141
basket flower, 46
beard-tongue, 47, 78
berlandiera lyrata, 60
Big Bend penstemon, 48
black-eyed susan, 49
blackfoot daisy, 50
blazing stars, 74
blood flower, 51
blue grama, 17
blue larkspur, 98
blue-eyed grass, 33, 52
bluebells, 33, 39, 53
bluebonnet, 7, 8, 9, 10, 11, 12, 13,
    16, 19, 23, 26, 29, 31, 32, 33,
    36, 37, 54
    Abbott pink, 14
    albino, 13
    Big Bend, 15
    red, 13, 14
    lavendar, 14

maroon, 14
pink, 13, 14
white, 13, 14
Brewster county, 8
buffalo clover, 7, 9
buffalo grass, 17, 24
buttercups, 96
butterfly, 31
    larvae, 32
butterfly-pea, 95
butterfly weed, 55
button flower, 73
button snakeroot, 107
cactus, 7, 24
callirhoe species, 142
calyptocarpus vialis, 124
cancer-weed, 56
capsicum annuum, 59
castilleja indivisa, 80
cedar, 23
celestial lily, 58
centaurea americana, 46
chile piquin, 59
chocolate flower, 60
clitoria mariana, 95
clover, 17
Comanche village, 9
commelinantia anomala, 70
compass plant, 61
Connally, John, 10
cooperia drummondii, 106
coral bean, 62
coreopsis, 32
coreopsis tickseed, 63
coreopsis tinctoria, 63
corydalis auera, 112
cotton, 7, 8
cupleaf pentsemon, 64
cut-leaved daisy, 68
datura inoxia, 83
dead-heading, 31, 32
delphinium carolinianum, 98